How To Start

A PROFITABLE WORM BUSINESS

ON A Shoestring Budget

By Stephan Kloppert

May 2013

Books may be purchased at

Amazon.com, www.worm-composting-help.com, selected bookstores and by contacting the publisher and author at:

Email: skadler888@yahoo.com

Cover Design: SRK Publications
Interior Design: SRK Publications
Publisher: SRK Publications
Edited by: Dinisha Sigamoney and Caroline Kloppert

ISBN: 978-0-620-57583-6
First Edition
Printed in the USA

TABLE OF CONTENTS

INTRODUCTION

Do you want to start a profitable worm business on a very small budget and in a limited space, but don't know how and where to start?

No need to look any further!
This book will tell you step by step, with easy to follow instructions, all you need to know about starting a profitable worm business from scratch!

I will share from my wealth of experience of more than 15 years as a worm farmer and worm business entrepreneur. Regardless of whether you just want to make some pocket money with a single worm-bin selling bait worms; or whether you want to create a full-time income for you and your family, you will learn proven low cost methods to start a worm business and make your mark in the constantly growing market of the worm farming industry.

When I told friends and family in 1998 that I intended to start a business breeding and selling worms in my backyard many of them probably thought that I was just a few French fries short of a happy meal!

Can one really make money with worms?
The answer is a resounding "**yes**!"

I make a living by breeding, growing and selling worms as well as other supplementary products in and from my backyard, and have done so for more than a decade now!

There are a lot of passionate people who have built up flourishing businesses by farming earthworms, and I wish them all the best and continued success!

I make no claim that my methods are the only way to succeed, but we have worked with worms successfully for many years now and I am sure that

A mature compost worm (Eisenia fetida)

this book will show you what methods and tools you need to start a profit making worm business of your own. As the title of this book states the main focus is to show low cost options to raise and sell worms to people that would love to create some extra income but have very limited funds to invest into a new business opportunity. If you can't invest a lot of cash but have the enthusiasm to make things happen you can start a successful worm business on a surprisingly low budget! You can work on your worm

A worm bed in a backyard

farming project part time or full time; keep it small so you can handle it alone or with a partner; or you can grow it into a big venture. A worm farmer doesn't need to be a technical genius or have loads of space to succeed! With a little area

like a cellar, garage or backyard, some discipline and the determination to succeed, anyone can make it happen!

5

Once you have read this book you should be able to:

- Raise and multiply earth worms (*Eisenia fetida and Eisenia andrei*)
- Build your own functional and commercially marketable worm farm(s)
- Know what to feed your worms and where to get the food for very little money or possibly for free
- Protect your worms against the elements and their natural predators
- Produce and harvest worm castings (potentially the world's richest organic fertilizer)
- Produce worm tea and worm leachate (liquidized worm castings)
- Know how to package, price, brand and deliver your worms and worm related products
- Offer work-shops to the public and potential clients that explain the basics of worm composting
- Build a range of commercially marketable worm farms
- Market your worm farms, worms, worm castings and worm tea to millions of potential customers, i.e. nurseries, garden centers, fishermen, gardeners, pet owners, private households (that want to recycle their food and garden scraps), restaurants, guesthouses, hotels, zoos...! The list goes on and on!
- Generate an income and run a profitable worm farming business

So let's get you started and on the way to becoming a successful worm-farming entrepreneur!

A 3-tier worm farm suitable for a 3-4 person household

A mature compost worm

Specific words and definitions

While you work your way through the chapters of this book you might learn about some definitions and words

A small worm farm for dog owners

used in worm farming that are new to you.

If you want to find out more about the worm-specific terminology, tools and accessories, or information one should know about worms and worm farming - take a look at the *Glossary* section at the end of this book for clarification. Alternatively, keep reading and refer to the *Glossary* at a later stage.

ESSENTIALS FOR WORM FARMING

How much space is required to start a worm farming business?
To start a worm farming business you do not need loads of space. A worm-composting project can easily be started in a storeroom, garage, garden or back yard.

There are obviously a few requirements that you need to meet to guarantee a smooth and satisfactory working process. Have a look at the list below to get an idea of the initial space requirements for your worm farming business. We are working on the potential requirements for 10 breeder bins with 1000 mature worms in each bin and a 5m square bulk bed. This set up should enable you to have between 60,000 to 70,000 worms on your worm farm at any given time. This should be a sufficient population to enter the market on a modest scale without depleting your supply of worms through sales. To achieve this production capacity you will need approximately:

1 x Bulk bed	5m²
10 x Breeder bins	3m²
Composting area	4m²
Worm food storage	2m²
Working table/s	2m²
Space for equipment	3m²
Space for products	5m²
Space for bottles	1m²
Packaging area	2m²
Packaging materials	½m²
Desk and office space	3m²

This is only a guideline. If you plan your project well you could start with even less than 30 square meters to get your worm business going.

You can expand later in accordance with the needs of your business.

PLANNING THE WORM FARMING PROJECT

What are the essentials?

To get the ball rolling and your worm farming business on its way you will just need 4 basic components:

- Worm bedding
- Worm food
- Worm bins /boxes /farms
- Worms

Study this chapter carefully as it contains the bulk of knowledge you need to have to successfully establish your worm business.

Let's have a closer look at each of the 4 key components of any worm farming business:

Worm bedding

- What can be used as bedding?
- How can it be obtained or prepared?

Worm bedding is an essential component of any worm bin. It provides protection as a safe retreat to which your worms can migrate from other areas of the bin, such as the upper level where the food is placed.

The environmental conditions in the food layer can become temporarily uncomfortable or even life threatening for worms for many reasons. For example, excessive heat created by the rotting process, or over acidity or souring of the food that has been added can be harmful!

Another problem that would force your worms to retreat to lower safer layers of a worm bin could be the lack of moisture near the surface area of the bin.

Any of the above mentioned situations would animate your worms to dig down deeper into the bedding. Worms will be able to process food that is too acidic to live in, as long as they have an area of safe bedding to retreat to after their meal.

There are many different materials that you can use to prepare safe bedding for your worm bins. Amongst the most popular are:

- Horse manure with or without straw or wood shavings
- Cattle manure with straw
- Sheep manure with straw
- Rabbit manure
- Shredded cardboard
- Shredded or torn up newspaper
- Garden compost
- Nutrient rich topsoil

A bucket with soaked newspaper strips

Worms in a piece of corrugated cardboard

All these materials make excellent safe bedding and most of them should be available at a very low cost or no cost at all. If you have farms nearby just call them and ask if you could assist them with their waste management by collecting some of their cow, sheep, horse, or rabbit manure. If you are lucky and negotiate well, some farmers or horse owners might even pay you to collect their organic waste, or deliver it to your property free of charge.

If you live in an urban area and have no access to any of the above-mentioned manures, or legislation does not permit the use of manure in your area, then use shredded cardboard or shredded or torn up newspaper for worm bedding.

It shouldn't be a problem to convince friends, family and neighbor's to keep their old newspapers for you. Another option is to contact local shops and ask them to keep their old cardboard boxes for you. Just see which material is the easiest to get hold of and which material you enjoy working with.

All the materials can be used on their own as bedding - if prepared properly beforehand. If you run short of any one of the materials, then they can be mixed together as well.

We at Global Worming work mostly with pure horse droppings, horse manure with straw, kitchen and garden waste and occasionally with shredded cardboard and paper. If you work with any of the manures, droppings or mixes of manures, it is recommended that you compost the material before you use it as bedding or as food source for your worms. There are several advantages to doing this:

- The composting process heats the manure up to a temperature of 80° C which will destroy any weed seeds and pathogens that are in the material. This will result in much cleaner and better worm castings that will fetch a higher price with your clients.
- Manures that have been fully composted can act as both worm bedding and worm food and will not endanger your worms by uncontrolled heating!

- Composted manures produce very nutrient rich worm castings.

Composting is not a difficult process. The following is a description of an easy composting style you can use to prepare your worm bedding and worm feeds.

Aerobic composting of worm bedding materials
Accessories needed for composting:

- One or two heavy duty plastic sheets – minimum size 3m x 3m
- A manure fork and or spade
- Bricks or planks to keep the plastic sheet in place
- A composting area of at least 2.5m x 2.5m which, for the sake of easy access, should not be against a wall and should be on a level or slightly elevated area (a low spot on your property might catch all the rain water which would make your composting efforts fail!)

Every compost heap needs water and air for bacteria and

A compost heap covered with plastic sheets

microorganisms to break down the manure or other organic matter. It is important to find the right balance between the different elements; otherwise the composting process will not work.

All of the manures mentioned above should be rinsed well. The water will remove excess urine, ammonia and harmful salts out of the bedding material and add the moisture needed for composting. Place the horse droppings or other manure in a woven bag in basin over a drain and rinse it with a hosepipe or a few buckets of water.

Then let the manure drain properly. Once liquids stop dripping out of the bag or bucket it should have the perfect moisture level and be ready for composting.

When you have formed your compost heap on your composting site cover it immediately. This is vital for the success of the process.

As I mentioned before, a strong sheet of plastic will do just fine for this. The cover keeps the moisture that is needed inside your compost heap and keeps rain or snow out.

In order to get the necessary oxygen to the bacteria and microorganisms in the compost heap, you have to turn/mix the compost heap every 4 to 5 days. It's quite a workout and that's why I suggest keeping your compost heaps small in the beginning. A pile of 1 to 1.5 cubic meters will be adequate for the process to work and is manageable!

To compost successfully perform the following steps:

- Add moist manure or other organic matter to your composting area until you have a heap of at least 1 cubic meter. Pile the materials up loosely without squeezing them together.
  This allows maximum oxygen penetration through your organic matter. Cover the heap with one or two plastic sheets making sure the sheet completely covers the pile. Use bricks or planks to hold the edges of the sheet down properly to prevent flies from getting into the manure and to keep the moisture inside.
  - Leave the manure pile undisturbed for 4 to 5 days.
  - Take off the plastic sheet in the morning. The pile should be heated up now due to the action of bacteria inside the heap.

Turn the composting material thoroughly with a manure fork or spade and cover it again with the plastic sheet.

- Wait for another 4 to 5 days then take off the plastic sheet in the morning, mix the heap again thoroughly and cover it again.
- Leave the manure pile undisturbed for another 4 to 5 days. Then remove the plastic sheet and check the size and temperature of the heap. It should have shrunk quite a bit (up to 50%) and there should no longer be any heat in the manure.
- If some of the material is still hot turn the heap one last time, cover it again with the plastic and wait for a couple of days.

Once the heat in the organic matter has completely disappeared, it is a clear indication that the manure has been fully composted and that it is now safe to use as bedding in your worm bins.

Using this method you can produce great bedding for your worms in just 12 to15 days. Another advantage is that composted manure has great nutritional value and can be used as a worm food source as well! We have worked with quite a few different materials to produce bedding, but over time have found that horse droppings or horse manure is the easiest to work with and usually available for free. If you can get hold of racehorse manure then go for it as they get treated like royalty and get the best food, which in turn will result in the best manure/droppings.

If you can't get hold of any manure then you should consider working with shredded newspaper and shredded cardboard. Both make an excellent starter bedding as well. If you want to work with paper it is best to stay away from the white paper used in copy machines and printers. It is sometimes too acidic and you might endanger your worm-herd.

It is best to use only old newspapers and cardboard boxes. Make sure to remove any shiny and glossy prints. If you use newspaper and cardboard, shred all the paper and cardboard before you soak it in water. Soak it for at least 12 hours then drain off the excess liquid and place a layer of about 10cm in either a breeding box or a bulk bed.

If you don't mind spending some additional money you can mix equal parts (50/50) of peat moss with any of the above mentioned bedding materials as well. Peat moss also needs to soak for at least 12 hours in water and after you have drained it properly you can mix it with the bedding material of your choice.
It is certainly a good way to produce safe bedding but we found that it is possible to work without the addition of peat moss. This will keep's the expenses down too!

Worm Food

- What do worms eat
- Where to get worm food
- How to get worm food for free
- How to get some money for taking or collecting worm food
- How to prepare the food and feed worms

There is one basic rule when it comes to worm food. Worms eat anything that has once been alive and is now dead! So all is food; from kitchen scraps (tea bags,

Most kitchen scraps can be used as worm food

coffee grounds, lettuce leaves) to human hair, garden waste, old fruit and animal waste. The list is virtually endless.

16

To view a list of worm foods go to http://www.worm-composting-help.com/Worm-food-rating-list.html. There you will find a regularly updated list of good and less desirable worm foods.

Worm foods are, in most cases, valuable organic materials that would probably end up on a landfill site if not used to feed to a worm-herd. The challenge for the worm farmer who wants to make a living with worms is to find a good food source that gives him continuous supply and is easy to work with. We found that although there is nothing wrong with adding kitchen scraps to your worm farms, the supply is usually limited and if they are not covered properly, they might attract a lot of flies.

In order to run your worm farm smoothly you should get food that is easy to handle and comes in limitless supply! Among the best solutions are pure horse droppings; horse manure with wood shavings or straw; rabbit manure; and horse-cattle-sheep-rabbit manure mixed with shredded cardboard.

Pure horse droppings
This is one of our preferred worm foods, available free of charge from many horse stables. The manure needs to be soaked in water and drained, to be ready for your worms to eat. Only a thin layer of food - not more than 10cm should be added to the worm farms at one time.

Horse manure with wood shavings or straw
This is another excellent food source for worms. Like horse droppings it is usually available free of charge from horse stables and riding schools. Again, only a thin food layer - not more than 10cm at a time should be added to the worm farms. This also needs to be soaked in water and drained to be ready for consumption.

Warning! Please note that horse owners might regularly treat their animals with medication to de-worm them.
Never feed your worms with horse droppings or horse manure from horses that have been given anti worm medication the day before.
Some of the medication could pass into their droppings and urine and could prove lethal to your worms if they ate them.

Speak to your supplier and stress this point to make sure you never get manure that might kill your worm-herd. The same precautions should be taken when feeding any waste produced by other animals.

Rabbit manure
Add a 10cm layer of food on top of your bedding. The manure should get treated the same way as horse droppings before you can feed it to your worms.
Rabbit manure is a really good worm food and you might want to look into the possibility of breeding rabbits on your worm farm as well. Make some additional money with the rabbits, which are considered a delicacy in many parts of the world.

Horse-cattle-sheep-rabbit manure mixed with shredded Cardboard
Add a 10cm food layer of this mix to the top of your bedding. The manure and cardboard should be soaked and drained before being added to the worm beds.

Note: If you want to add a thicker layer of food to your worm beds it is important to remember that the material might heat up if it has not been completely composted!
Note: To avoid potential harm to your worms, as a safety measure you should never cover the surface area of any of your worm bins, big or small, completely with food. When you add food to a

breeder bin cover one half of the bins surface only and next time you add food use the other half of the bin.

When adhering to this rule you give your worms a chance to migrate to the food-free side of the worm bin should there be anything harmful or threatening in the food you recently added. Whenever you add fresh food make it a habit to check briefly the next morning if the worms are ok. Should they all be on the food-free side of the bin, on the surface or the sides of the bin you can be sure that the food wasn't ok. (Check the troubleshooting chapter for help).

You might need a permit for using manure on your premises. Find out what is allowed by your local municipality or the Department of Environmental Affairs. There are a lot of other kinds of worm foods that are quite good and that might be readily available in your hometown, which you could use without requiring any permits. Worm food can be obtained from grocery stores, fruit and vegetable markets, food processing plants, restaurants, corporate kitchens, hotels, guesthouses and farms.
This list, although incomplete, shows that there are many options available for you to get hold of food for your worms.
Many producers of organic materials will gladly give you their food or animal wastes for free and, if you negotiate well, **some might even be prepared to pay you** to collect their waste products from their premises.

They have to get rid of the organic matter on a regular basis and will be glad if you assist them in this task. So if you are prepared to go the extra mile, place an advert in your local classifieds and contact potential worm food producers to see if you can strike a deal with them. Offer them a waste collection service. If your services are cheaper than those of other contractors you might get the job and actually make money collecting the food you need for your worms. Just remember that worms always prefer moist food so if it doesn't have enough moisture on its own you need to soak the food in water and then drain the excess liquid off before feeding it to the worms.

If you mix 2 or more feeds it's best to blend them together before you soak them. Any of the above organic materials mentioned would be great worm food on its own or mixed with one or several of the others. Just do a little research and you'll find a good and constant food supply for your worm business.

Worm food for bait sized worms

Worms that are fattened to serve as bait for recreational fishermen are in high demand in many parts of the world and fetch higher prices than worms from normal bulk beds that are smaller or come in a variety of sizes. In order to get the worms

Adding dog poop to a fattening bin

to grow big and plump you will have to treat them differently to your worms in standard bulk beds. To fatten worms to top sizes you want them to feed heavily on high protein feeds and live in a wetter than usual environment. When you start out it would probably be best to begin with just a few smaller bins in order to get a feel for it but once your demand starts growing you can apply the same feeding principles to a bulk bed prepared especially for fattening worms.

Many worm farmers swear by ground poultry mash or other ground feeds to fatten worms and they probably work. We haven't used them because they have to be purchased at a considerable cost and we found two food sources that work just as well if not better than any other food to produce big juicy worms. Both are either freely available or cost next to nothing.

Our preferred fattening foods are:

- Dog poop and
- Air dried aged sewage sludge

Yes you might wrinkle your nose right now but we've used dog poop particularly as the sole food source for bait worms for many years now and achieved excellent results. With dogs being

A simple box with a lid can be used as a fattening bin.

probably the most popular pets worldwide you might have one or two of them yourself. If not there will surely be some dogs in your neighborhood! I have three dogs and they are producing loads and loads of waste or top class worm food on a daily basis!

Sewage sludge should be air dried and aged for at least 6 to 9 months to make sure there are no harmful pathogens left in it. It is usually readily available from your municipality and should be either free of charge or can be purchased at a minimal cost.

Worms

There are thousands of different kinds of earthworms but very few of them are commercially usable. The kind of worm we are working with is known by many different names, depending where in the world you are living.

A compost worm can reach a length of 20 centimeters

Tiger worms, red worms, red wrigglers or composting worms are just some of the names they go by. In order to identify them correctly we have to call them by their *Latin* name that is the same all over the world. The worm to use for your worm farming business is *Eisenia fetida/Eisenia foetida* or its close cousin, *Eisenia andrei*. These worms can eat about half their bodyweight per day in captivity, are hardy and best of all, tend to be prolific breeders.

Multiplication of worms under ideal circumstances

Under ideal circumstances your worm population could double every 2 to 3 months. So if you start with just 1000 mature worms you can have more than 3 Million worms within 1 year. That is way more than you will need to start your business. The table on the following page will give you an idea of how quickly you can multiply your worm-herd to a number that will enable you to open shop and start making some money with your project.

These calculations were based on only 2 cocoons being produced by each mature worm per month with an average of 3 infant worms hatching out of each cocoon after about 27 days.

Possible multiplication figures of compost worms

MONTH	MATURE WORMS	TOTAL WORMS	HATCHED WORMS	COCOONS
1	1 000	1 000	0	2 000
2	1 000	7 000	6 000	2 000
3	1 000	13 000	6 000	2 000
4	1 000	19 000	6 000	2 000
5	7 000	25 000	6 000	14 000
6	13 000	67 000	42 000	26 000
7	19 000	145 000	78 000	40 000
8	25 000	265 000	120 000	50 000
9	77 000	415 000	150 000	154 000
10	155 000	877 000	462 000	310 000
11	275 000	1 807 000	930 000	550 000
12	425 000	3 457 000	1 650 000	850 000

The numbers speak for themselves and show how quickly you can build up your stock if everything works out perfectly. But this is rarely the case under normal circumstances. You will lose some worms to predators, some will migrate out of your bins and others might die if the bedding is too dry or acidic.

Anyway, you certainly will not need millions of worms to establish yourself as a worm farmer. I suggest you build up a mature worm population of about 10000 to 13000 worms, which will give you a monthly output of at least 60000 worms. This is a manageable amount and will allow you to enter the market confidently.
Keep in mind that you must not sell worms from your breeder boxes unless you are replacing them with new breeders! They are the engine of your business and will continually supply you with new infant worms for several years!
To start off with, you should obtain at least 500 to 1000 worms

There are a few options you can choose from to obtain your first batch of worms. You can either go to Google or any search engine of your choice and type in keywords like earthworms for sale, composting worms for sale, worm farms, etc.
Then search for a worm breeder in your hometown or country and place your order.

Many worm suppliers post or courier their worms. We do it as well and they travel either in safe insulated containers or simple plastic bags filled with safe bedding that will support them easily for up to 4 weeks. So it is usually no problem to order your wiggly friends online and have them sent to you.
Before you order worms compare the prices of at least 2 or 3 suppliers so that you do not pay more than you need to.
To get the breeding off the ground, you should order at least 500 worms, which are a good starter population for one breeder bin.

I am sure that you can get a starter batch of worms in your town or country for less than you would spend eating out one evening.

If you don't want to use the internet search engines to find a supplier you can try the worm-business-directory at http://www.worm-composting-help.com/worm-business-directory.html which is continuously growing and might help you to find a worm farmer in your country or town. Once you have started your worm business just let me know and your worm farm could get listed in the worm business directory as well.

However if you do have the time and patience to start your worm business at a slower pace you might even be able to get your starter batch of worms without spending a dime!

If you have a compost heap in your garden or backyard have a look at it. If it is in a good condition (check the chapter on composting for details), you might find loads of compost worms in it having a feast.

If you don't have a compost heap yourself, spread the word and ask friends and family to look in their compost heaps. The worms you might find there will probably be compost worms of the type *Eisenia fetida*.

Collect them and place in a bin or bucket with some safe bedding and you are in business. Once you have set up your first breeding bin you will be ready to multiply your worm-herd.
Let's have a look at the breeding behavior of *Eisenia fetida* worms to find out why worm multiplication happens so rapidly.

Breeding behavior and breeding cycle
Compost worms are hermaphrodites and possess both male and female sex organs. The good news for us worm farmers is that worms are not picky at all when it comes to choosing a suitable partner.

As a matter of fact they will basically mate with any mature worm that crosses their path. Once two adult worms meet they will face each other and attach their male sexual organ to the female sexual organ of their partner. When they separate, they will part ways and fertilize their eggs with the sperm they received from their mating partner. Both worms will have fertilized eggs.

The clitellum - the thick band containing the eggs or cocoon, located not far behind the head of the mature worm - will visibly swell.

The 2 worms in this picture are mating. This process can take several hours

Within 4 days the worms will shed the swelling round their clitellum as a cocoon or egg capsule and will be ready to mate again. Mature worms usually mate between 2 to 4 times per month. Under favorable conditions

Fresh cocoons are beige in color and about the size of a pinhead

the cocoons containing infant worms have an incubation period of about 27 days. After that period an average of 2 to 4 infant worms will hatch. The baby worms will grow rapidly and become mature worms in about 2 to 3 months.

Multiplying your worm-herd

In order to get ready to do business you obviously have to take action and help your worms to multiply. To get your first breeder box into production you should ideally have at least 500 mature worms to work with.

Briefly glance through the bedding of your first batch of worms to get an idea of the quantity of mature worms it contains. If you are not certain that you have at least 500 mature worms to start your first breeder box then don't worry counting them. Either find or order some more worms or just put all the mature *and* infant worms that you have into a prepared breeder bin and give them about 60 to 90 days to mature and multiply.

A breeder box should be covered with plastic to keep moisture inside

During this time you must make sure that the conditions in your worm bin will remain ideal for the worms to grow and breed.

When you are confident that you have sufficient stock of mature worms in your worm bin place the contents of the bin on your working table and carefully spread out some of the bedding till you have a thin layer of about 1 - 2cm in thickness.

Search for mature worms within the spread out bedding and place them in your first breeder box filled with safe bedding. Add at least 500 mature worms to the bin. If you have sufficient stock of mature worms set up more breeder boxes with 500 to 1000 worms each.

Add some food to each breeder box, cover the surface with a protective cover and give the worms 21 to 25 days to breed. Left over immature worms can be added to your bulk bed and given more time to grow.

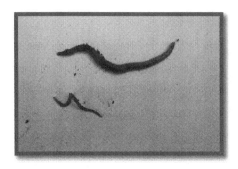

2 young worms- One just a couple of days-, the other one a few weeks old

After 3 weeks take each of the breeder boxes again and separate mature worms from the infant ones. Put the mature worms back into their old bins with fresh bedding. Start a new breeding bin with the bedding containing the infant worms and cocoons. Most of these infant worms and cocoons should be mature after 60 to 90 days and start producing their own offspring.

Repeat this cycle every 21 to 25 days till you have 10 breeder boxes prepared. Once you have 10 breeder boxes stocked with 500 to 1000 mature worms each harvest the infant worms and cocoons every 21 to 25 days and add them to your bulk bed/s. This keeps the density of adult worms in the breeder boxes low so that breeding rates stay high.

Working with 10 breeder boxes is of course only a suggestion. Adapt the concept mentioned above to your personal needs and goals. If you have the time and want to build up your business slowly, just work with 5 breeder boxes or whichever number will suit you.

No matter how small or big you start you can always accelerate or slow down your production within a short period of time.

Harvesting worms from bulk beds

After you have stocked your bulk bed/s with infant worms from your breeder boxes for 2 months you should be able to harvest worms for the first time.

Ideally you should have at least 2 bulk beds so that you can alternate your harvesting activities between them. This will give the worms in the beds some time to eat, grow and multiply undisturbed for a few weeks. We usually give our worm beds a rest of between 3 to 5 weeks before we harvest them again. It is entirely fine to work with only one bulk bed in the beginning. Two might not be possible initially, and not necessary if you plan on only selling a limited amount of worms at first.

A week before harvesting from a bulk bed, add a 10cm or 4 inch layer of fresh food over a 1 - 2m area. Place the food on top of the bedding and cover the bed immediately.

A pile of bedding with worms

On the day you want to harvest, get up early in the morning before the sun heats up, take your manure fork and remove the top 15 cm of feed and bedding from the harvesting area. Place this top layer in buckets or a wheelbarrow.

Worms are top feeders and many of them will be in the vicinity of the fresh food that you added just a few days before.

Another reason to do this in the morning is the fact that worms are most active in the early hours of the day.

You should see a lot of worms while you are filling up the buckets. Don't try to get all of them. There will be plenty of worms in your

Bedding gets removed from the pile containing the worms

harvesting containers. Cover the bulk bed as you would normally do and take your buckets of worm rich bedding to your working table. There are quite a few ways of counting worms.

Some farmers weigh them and sell them by weight, which is a practice we don't implement because we found that it caused the worms too much stress and in some instances even harmed them.

In order to weigh them you have to manually separate the worms from their bedding, which is achieved by taking advantage of the worm's dislike or fear of light. A worm picker will place a cone shaped

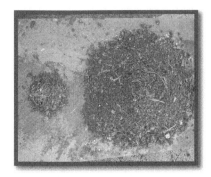

Worms (left) separated from bedding (right)

pile of worm rich bedding on a worktable that is exposed to the light of a lamp or the sun.

Then he waits about 5 minutes to give the worms time to dive deeper into their bedding trying to escape from the light. After five minutes the worm picker will remove some bedding from the outside of the pile that will be free of worms. Once he has taken off enough bedding to see some worms again he will stop and wait for another 5 to 10 minutes.

After repeating this process several times the worms will be left with less and less bedding to hide in until the worm picker ends up with a pile of worm bedding on one side of the table and on the other side a ball of worms all bunched up trying to escape from the light by wriggling together.

Now the worms should be weighed and placed in a sales container with safe bedding as soon as possible.
It is very important to handle worms with care and spread them out over the bedding in the container. If this is not done it is possible that worms that are still sticking together will not untangle themselves and thus loose lots of moisture to their environment! This might actually kill a lot of worms in a short time. Worms that die in confined spaces with limited air circulation can endanger the other worms inside the container by the gases (ammonia) they give off as they decompose, leading to mass death of the worms.
This is a terrible experience and the bad odor produced by the dead worms in a confined space is something one does not want to experience often.
At *Global Worming* we decided years ago to pick and count the worms that are going on sale. This sounds a little weird at first, and may appear to be a slow process but is actually not the case.

A good worm picker can count up to 2000 worms per hour if the setup is right and there are plenty of worms in the bedding he or she is working with.
Yes, it is true that there are many who would run away if you asked them to touch a worm. But if one considers that a worm picker should always work with gloves and that the worms are actually much less revolting than many people think, then it is not so surprising that there are more people prepared to do this job than you might initially think.

In practice it is vital to work quickly, carefully and efficiently when counting worms.

When you want to count worms for your sales stock it is important to have a good look at the place in the bulk bed that you want to harvest worms from. Remember that your worm beds always need some time to recover and multiply their worm stock after you have harvested them.

So it's quite a good practice to keep accurate records of your harvesting, adding of worms to beds and the feeding regime. If you manage your worm beds well, you will ensure that you always have plenty of worms in at least some areas of your worm farm.

When you have identified an area of your worm bed that you want to harvest, make sure that it has lots of worms in the bedding. You should see worms right below the cover when you lift it.
 If there are none, or just a few worms below the cover this will be a clear indication that the worm bed doesn't have enough worm stock yet and should not be harvested.

If there are only a few worms in the bedding it is advisable to rather go to a different place in your bulk bed to harvest worms.

Bedding that only holds a few worms will slow down the counting and increase your costs.

"Picking" method

The simplest way to pick and count worms is to place a manageable amount of worm rich bedding on a worktable, next to a small bucket with a capacity of 5 liters, and a larger bucket or bin below the work area. Now carefully spread out some of the bedding containing worms over the worktable till the layer of bedding is only about 1 - 2cm thick. You will be able to spot worms amongst the bedding. Carefully pick them up and place them (gently) in your 5-liter bucket that should already be filled with about 3 liters of safe bedding.

Initially you will have to concentrate quite a bit in order to see all the worms within the bedding because when they lie still they are difficult to spot in the compost. After a while you will get the hang of it and fill up a worm bucket in

A simple worm counting table

no time. Practice makes perfect! Count only the worms that have already reached a reasonable size of at least 3 - 4cm. Once the bedding that you have worked on is depleted of worms, brush the bedding still containing tiny worms and cocoons down into the big bucket below your worktable.

Spread out the next load of bedding and continue picking and counting. Initially you might only pick one worm at a time but after a while and with experience you will accurately guess if you have 3, 5, 10 or 20 worms between your fingers. Then you will be able to speed up your counting dramatically. Once you have reached your target amount of worms in your 5l bucket add another liter of safe bedding and place some worm food over half the surface area. Close the bucket with a tight-fitting lid that has 6 to 8 holes with a diameter of at least 5mm to allow good air circulation inside the bucket. We fill a 5-liter bucket with 500 worms and add 5 to 10 extra, which ensures that we supply the advertised amount of worms to our clients. You won't believe how many people have asked me over the years if I could guarantee that the advertised amount of worms was inside a worm bin or worm bucket.

Quite a few people have actually sat down and counted the worms they purchased to prove me wrong. Having hand counted the worms we can assure them that they got what they paid for and we never had comebacks since we started using this method.
500 worms that are supplied with proper safe bedding and food can live in a worm bucket comfortably for at least a month.
After that it is advisable to check if their bedding and food needs to be topped up and if the moisture level inside the bucket is still sufficient. If needed make the necessary adjustments and place the bucket back into the storage space.
I'll go into more detail about the storing of worms in sales containers in a later chapter of this book, when I introduce you to the different kinds of products and potential markets for your worm business.

"Reduce the piles" method

The hand counting method can of course be refined in different ways to speed up production. The first option is to form several cone shaped piles of worm rich bedding either under a light or outside in the sun.
Once the cones are formed wait for 5 to 10 minutes and then apply the same method of bedding removal that I mentioned earlier in this chapter. In the meantime you can do some other work or count worms from another pile. Take off some bedding every 5 to 10 minutes until you have removed about half or even three quarters of the bedding from each cone.

This process will only take you a few minutes of actual labor but the reduced bedding you have to work with later will speed up your worm picking considerably.

Sieve method

Another way to speed up the counting process is by using a frame with walls   5 – 10cm high, attached to a mesh with holes. The size of the holes should not exceed 2.5cm in diameter. The mesh can be made out of wire or plastic but mustn't have sharp edges that could injure the worms.

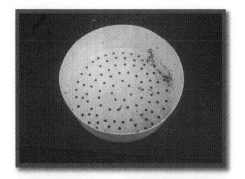

The way to work with the sieve is as follows: Place the sieve on your working table. Sprinkle a few handfuls of worm rich bedding onto the sieve and carefully shake it. The

Fine particles on the right have fallen through the sieve

thin particles of the bedding will fall through the holes while the larger pieces and the worms stay behind (See picture above). Now pick up the worms as they become exposed and place them in your sales bucket. They will be easier to spot with the reduced amount of bedding inside the sieve. The finer the bedding you use the quicker the worm harvest will progress with this method.

Worm harvester method

This is probably the fastest but also the most expensive way of harvesting worms. It is especially costly for a beginner. It's not really for those that want to start their business on a shoestring

35

A worm harvester

budget but nevertheless I will briefly share this method with you. A worm harvester helps to separate large volumes of worm castings, worm food and worms in a very short time. What essentially happens is that you throw worm rich bedding into the opening on the upper side of the worm harvester that rotates continuously.

There are different kinds of mesh along the cylindrical body of the harvester that will allow the castings, bedding, cocoons and small worms to fall through the holes into holding containers below the machine, while the large worms will travel down to the end of the machine where they can be easily harvested. In this way you are actually harvesting worms and worm castings at the same time.

There are quite a few suppliers offering these harvesters especially in the United States, but the cost for one machine is at least $3000 (excluding transport).

I believe a worm harvesting machine is not needed for success when starting out, so don't worry if you cannot afford one of these machines. You can run your worm business without one for quite some time. If you want one of those machines but would like to save on costs, try to build one yourself or ask a friend to assist you. We built our worm harvester ourselves and it definitely saved us a nice sum of money.

Restocking bulk beds

No matter which method of worm harvesting you decide to use, remember to restock bulk beds that you have harvested regularly.

A good way to do this is to replace large worms that you have removed from a bulk bed and stored for sale, with bedding that contains infant worms and cocoons harvested from your breeder boxes.

We do this on a daily basis! In the morning go to the bulk beds you want to harvest, fill your buckets with worm rich bedding and cover the beds again. In the afternoon, add new hatchlings and cocoons that you have harvested from your breeder boxes, with their bedding, into the same bulk bed.

Then top it up with some fresh food. The food will protect the infant worms and cocoons from potential danger and will give lots of nourishment in the near future.

A bulk bed that has been harvested extensively and refilled with fresh worms and cocoons from your breeder bins should be left to recuperate for at least 21 days.

Worm bins

Worm bins are containers that ensure that worms will have a comfortable home to live in. They do not have to be fancy canisters or crates. Worms are not fussy and will make themselves at home in virtually any container that will meet their basic requirements. In order to feel comfortable, compost worms need:

- *Protection against extreme temperatures -*
  Good places for your bin are a shady place in the garden under a tree or bush, a storeroom, the garage, a cellar or a shaded terrace.
- *Protection against flooding -*
  Water build-up in a worm farm can cause the worms to leave their bin or drown. You should drill drainage holes of 6 - 8mm into the bottom of your bin to allow excess liquids to run off.

- *Protection against the sun -*
  Shade cover is a must: Place worm farms under a roof, a tree or inside a storeroom. Always cover your bins with a lid.
- *Protection against natural predators -*
  (See section on Pests and Predators)
- *Worm bedding -*
  The bedding serves as living- and breeding space for worms.
- *Correct moisture level of their environment -*
  Bedding that is roughly as moist as a squeezed out sponge is perfect. A little wetter is still ok. If in doubt rather have the bedding too wet than too dry!
- *Food -*
  Any suitable organic material worms can feed on.

As a worm farmer there are different kinds of worm bins that you should work with to get a productive worm business going.

- Breeding bins
- Bulk beds
- Fattening bins and
- Fattening bulk beds

Breeding bins and bulk beds are absolutely essential for your worm farming business. You can add fattening bins and possibly fattening bulk beds at a later stage when you are ready to cater for the bait market!

Breeding Bins
Once you get your first batch of worms you have to set up some breeding bins, which will be the engine of your worm farming business. They should be stocked with 500 to 1000 mature worms of breeding size that will consistently produce infant worms for you. If you are not fussy, any old container out of wood, plastic,

metal or bricks with a volume of at least 10 liters should keep your worms happy. Have a look around the house or ask family and friends for some containers that you can use on your premises. The cheapest worm bins that can be used as breeding bins are

Stacked breeding bins

These bins with closed sides are our preferred breeder boxes. Light, stackable and retaining the moisture of the bedding

simple plastic shopping bags that you usually get at any grocery store. We used them initially as an experiment and they worked exceptionally well and have lasted for a really long time. Some have been in use for more than 18 months now and they are still going strong! To turn a plastic bag into a worm bin just fill some safe bedding into the bag, add worms and then place worm food on top. Close the bag with one loose knot and hang the worm farm onto a hook or a nail.

If you want to see some of those worm bins (bags) in action have a look at my article at http://www.worm-composting-help.com/crazy-worm-bin.html
Although there is nothing wrong with using plastic bags and different kinds of containers, you should as well consider working with stackable breeding bins. This will save you time and space. We

found them to be ideal breeding bins. Each bin should be able to hold at least 500 mature breeding worms.

We use different kinds of breeding bins but the most convenient size we work with is 49cm in length by 35cm in width and 20cm in height (See picture on previous page). It's big enough to hold 1000 breeders and still small enough to be handled by an individual person. You might not be able to get this size of bin in your area but it is only meant to be a guideline. Bigger bins can become very heavy and difficult to handle for a single person.

If you don't have suitable bins at home and can't get them through family or friends, you might be able to get some you can

Food added to a bulk bed that is placed against a concrete wall

convert into breeding bins at a plastic-container recycler or a scrap yard.

Place a free advert in your local online junk mail / classifieds. If all else fails go to your local plastic warehouse and search for bins you can use as breeding bins. Keep in mind that a purchased breeding bin should last for at least 5 to 6 years. So make sure you get bins that are durable.

Worms are not fussy so any reject boxes with stains or small flaws that you can get for a fraction of their normal price will be just fine.

Bulk beds

Bulk beds are bigger worm bins that can be anything from 3m² to 100m².

They must be stocked regularly with worms that come from your breeding bins. The worms in your bulk beds will convert their bedding and food into nutrient rich worm castings and will grow until they are ready to be sold to your customers. Bulk beds come in many shapes and sizes. You can make them out of bricks, wooden boards, concrete, old bathtubs, metal or just an opaque durable plastic sheet.

Bulk beds should be around 1m wide and ideally be accessible from at least one side, so that you can comfortably work on them without having to stand on the bedding and worms.

Although a bin built out of bricks looks really attractive and works well too it's quite fine to work with bulk beds made out of plastic sheets initially. Plastic sheets are quite reasonably priced and usually available at hardware stores or warehouses that supply the building and construction trade. They are sold by the running meter. The ideal width to purchase is 3m. Slightly narrower sheeting will work as well.

As I mentioned earlier, you can make your bulk bed as small or as big as you like but we found that a good bulk bed for a new worm business should be about 5m long and 1m wide. For a bulk bed of that size you need to buy a plastic sheet at least 7m in length and 3m in width. The extra length and width of the plastic is essential to keep the environment favorable for your worm-herd.

When looking for a good spot for your bulk bed remember it should ideally be in a spot that doesn't get too much sun in the middle of the day. Once you have decided where to place your bulk bed make sure that the ground is level. If no level ground is available a slightly sloped area will be fine as well.

Remove any objects that can interfere with the plastic sheet like glass, rocks, bricks, sticks, tree-stumps, bushes etc., from the ground and place your 'sheet' with its center over the allocated area. Your plastic sheet should be approximately 1m bigger than your bulk bed on all 4 sides.

Now take an old screwdriver or ice pick and punch holes 20 – 30cm apart into an area measuring 5m x 1m in the middle of the sheet, in preparation for the worm bedding. These holes are there to make sure any excess water will drain off. If you punch in a few holes more or less, that will not be a

Worm bedding on a plastic sheet

problem.

Fill the center of your plastic sheet with your safe bedding to a height of at least 30 cm, then fold over all 4 open sides, starting with the ends first and then the 2 long sides. Your bedding should now be wrapped like a parcel.

A finished bulk bed

Cover the top with an old carpet. It works as protection for the plastic against heat from the sun. Let it stand undisturbed for 48 hours then open the sheet and check the temperature. If it has heated up it's a clear indication that the bedding hasn't been completely composted. You will have to wait for another 2 to 3 days till the bedding has cooled down before you can add your first lot of worms.

Never add worms to worm bedding that is hot. Composting material can heat up to 80 °C. If the worms can't find areas that are cooler in your worm bed, they will either leave the bed or die!

Once you are sure that there are no heated areas in the bedding dig a small trench about 10cm deep, 10cm wide and 50cm long, along the middle of the surface of your worm bin. Now add infant worms, cocoons and bedding that you got from your breeder

boxes to the trench. Cover again with bedding and add some freshly soaked and drained worm food over roughly half of your bulk bed. Close all 4 open sides of the plastic sheet as before; cover the top with the old carpet again and leave the bulk bed undisturbed for 4 days.

On the morning of the 5th day open the plastic cover and see if there is some worm activity. If you see a few worms on the surface of the bedding right after you open it that is a good sign and indicates that the worms are happy in their new home and have started to consume the food.

Close the covers again and give the worms another week before you make the next spot check. Do this once a week without removing any worms. After 2 months the worms of the first batch you added to the bed should be ready for picking and selling.

Remember that you will regularly have to add new infant worms and capsules to your bulk bed to replace the sold worms and avoid a shortage of stock.

Fattening bins
You can set up your fattening bin in the same way as the breeder boxes or bulk beds. Make sure the fattening bin has sufficient

drainage holes about 10 cm above the bottom of the bin. Fill it with 15 – 20 cm of safe bedding and add a batch of approximately 500 different sized worms to the bin.

Give the worms time (10 - 15 minutes should do the trick) to dig down into the bedding and then add a layer of fresh dog poop over one half of your bin. Water the whole surface of the bin thoroughly and close the lid. Give the worms a few days to settle into their new home checking briefly, once a day, to see if they are doing well.

Monitor the changes inside the bin. After a week or so you should see the worm poop that you have added to the bin slowly sink down or dissolve. This is a result of the feeding action of your worms. Once the worms have become active add some more dog poop (the fresher the better). Ensure that you never cover the whole surface of the bin. Keep the poop and the bedding very moist by adding some water to it at least once every 14 days. After 30 days put on some rubber gloves and check the size and shape of your worms.
By now you should have a lot of big fat worms that would make excellent bait for freshwater fish. Once a healthy population of bait sized worms is established you can start selling baitworms. This will avoid overpopulation - restricting the size of the worms, or forcing them to migrate out of your bin.

When your bin is well established you will notice lots of worm capsules in the bedding as a result of their breeding activities. We found over the years that worms in bins fed with dog poop produced more cocoons than those in other bins. If you are producing way more bait worms than you can sell you should regularly reduce the worm population of your bin. You can take a good number, such as 500 to 1000 and either start a new breeder bin with them or move them to your bulk beds. This will ensure that the remaining worms will enjoy their stay in your fattening bin and grow quickly to bait sizes. If your demand for bait-sized worms outstrips your production capacity then simply start another bin!

Fattening bulk beds

If you feel the need to start a fattening bulk bed use the same set up as for a standard bulk bed. Instead of adding the staple bulk bed food, either add dog poop or air dried sewer sludge.

Note: If you are using sewer sludge it is vital to make sure that it has been aged for at least 6 to 9 months.

Give the worms 48 hours to settle in before you have a look at the conditions inside the bed. If you see that the worms are eating, make sure to add fattening food and water regularly to keep the worms constantly supplied with nutrients and living in the right conditions to grow nice and plump.

PROTECTION FROM THE ELEMENTS

As I mentioned before in the book, earthworms are generally pretty hardy but you have to make sure that some basic requirements are met for them to survive. They need to be protected from the sun, wind, natural enemies and extreme temperatures, that usually occur during summer and winter.

Summer protection
In the hot summer months worm bins and beds can overheat when exposed to the sun on very hot days. It is generally a good idea to set up breeder bins and bulk beds in an area where they will get as little sun as possible, or at least some shade.

There are many ways you can go about this.
You can place bins under trees, in a garage or storeroom, under a roof or in an alley that gets only some sun. Any place on your property that gets exposure to the sun for a limited time, either early morning or late afternoon, when the direct sunlight is not that strong, should be good enough.

If you are unable to utilize any of the options mentioned above, than you have to provide your worms with some custom built sun-protection.

Place the worms indoors for protection from extreme temperatures

Second hand carpets on top of a strong plastic sheet are a good and inexpensive solution. Old wooden boards will do as well. Flattened cardboard boxes may also be used but they will decompose with time and become food for the worms. In windy climates, they will need to be weighted down with bricks. Another alternative is to set up a roof made of the shade cloth that you can purchase from most large nurseries and garden suppliers.

This is obviously a more costly solution and not really necessary if one takes advantage of the low, or no cost, environmentally friendly, recycling solutions mentioned above.

Should the temperatures in the shade be above 28 ° C, than it becomes really dangerous for your worms. In this instance you should consider filling up your worm farm with as much bedding as possible. I would suggest a mixture of slightly moist compost and worm castings. This additional bedding will act as an insulator against extreme temperatures and might give the worms the opportunity to hide in the depths of the worm bed furthest away from the heat.

Another way to keep the bedding and worms from overheating would be to pour cold water over the worm bedding regularly, during the heat of the day. I would only suggest cooling the beds with water in emergencies, because apart from it being time consuming, the water will only be cool initially, and will warm up to be the same as the air temperature after a while. Thus soggy bedding can end up warmer than dryer bedding. So it is advisable to be careful with this method! But if your worm breeder boxes are correctly set up with drainage holes, this cooling process could work.

Proper aeration of worm bins is another important factor. The air inside the worm bin needs to have a way to get out of the bin to prevent it from overheating!

Another effect that the sun and persistent wind can have is that they might dry out the worm food and bedding which would force the worms to leave the worm bin or face certain death. That's why it is vital to always make sure that the moisture levels inside your worm bins are conserved and at optimum levels. This can be achieved quite successfully by covering the sides and the top with plastic, which will prevent the moisture from evaporating and protect your worms from the sun and wind.

Many bins have solid plastic walls and will only need a sheet of plastic to cover the worm food inside your worm bin. The plastic

sheet should preferably be opaque to protect the worms from sunlight but if the bins are placed in a shaded area clear plastic will be fine as well. If you have bins with open sides you will have to cover all the sides with plastic.

We found the best way to do this is to place a bag inside the bin and fold the top over the bedding containing your worms (as shown in the pictures on this page).

I am sure you will find a solution that works well with the kind of bins that you use. If everything else fails ask your partner to create some space in the refrigerator for a while! (Just kidding ☺)

Winter protection
This will obviously differ quite a lot depending on which climate zone of the world you live in.

In mild climate zones where the temperature never really drops below 5 °C, it is quite easy to keep your worms safe. To get your worm bins ready for winter just make sure that all of them contain enough bedding and food to give worms a protective barrier of at least 30cm on all sides. This will give your worm-herd the chance to crawl towards the center of their bedding which will act as an insulating material against the low temperatures outside. An additional carpet or blanket as cover over the top and sides of your bins will help as well. That is usually all it takes, apart from your usual routine, to get your worms safely through winter.

If it is not too cold your worms will still be producing a fair amount of cocoons and infant worms during this time. However if you are living in parts of the world with freezing cold winters where your worm bins are exposed to temperatures below 5 °C than you have to keep the bedding and food levels much higher than during summer.

Bedding material can act as an insulating agent and will allow worms to hide away from the cold.

Another good way to protect breeder bins against cold weather is a polystyrene box with lid. They are easy to make and work well.

If the bedding in your worm bins or bulk beds is too shallow a fall in temperature to below freezing point could destroy your entire worm-herd. So it is vital to prepare for the cold weather. It is advisable to move breeder boxes into an indoor facility that can be heated up if needed. This will ensure that you will have some stock that you can sell even in the cold winter months. Should you not have enough space to accommodate all your breeder boxes indoors than it would probably be best to add the contents to your winter outdoor bed to give them a better chance to survive the coldest time of the year.

A winter outdoor bed should be at least 1. 5m wide and extend down at least 50cm into the ground.

You will need 3 different kinds of organic materials for your winter bed:
- Safe bedding
- Partially composted material that has been turned once after 4 or 5 days and left for another 4 to 5 days before being used for the winter bed
- Fresh horse or cattle manure with straw, properly washed and drained. Should you not have access to manure use any compostable material of your choice

Decide on the size of the winter bed you want to set up and:
- Dig the trench at least 50cm into the ground. You can make the trench narrower than 1.5m to save some time and labor, but it should at least be 1m wide at the bottom
- Fill the trench to three quarters of its depth with standard safe bedding. Add your worms and give them some time to crawl down
- Next, fill up the rest of the trench with partially composted material that still has some heat in it. Once the trench is filled up keep adding more of the partially composted material to your winter bed till the pile of bedding has a height of about 30cm along the whole length of your bed
- Now top up with a 30cm layer of fresh horse manure mixed with straw or any compostable material of your choice
- Cover the bed completely with 2 sheets of plastic and 2 layers of carpet

- Secure the edges of the bed with bricks and leave undisturbed for up to 3 months

It is obviously important that all the different materials used for the bed have been treated properly as discussed in earlier chapters of this book. The two top layers should provide heat for some time and the bedding material will gradually become available as food for your worms during the course of the cold winter months. Should you live in an area that experiences long hard winters with repeated subfreezing temperatures you might have to consider the possibility of topping up the bed after about 2 to 3 months. Wait for a day with moderate temperatures and add some fresh horse manure or a compostable material of your choice to the top of the worm bed.

Once the dangers of extreme cold temperatures are over, you can open up the bed and commence with your standard bulk bed routine.

NATURAL ENEMIES

There are quite a lot of animals that can harm your worms such as birds, toads, frogs, centipedes, rats, ants, red mites and moles. Unfortunately the list is long and those mentioned are just some of the countless predators that enjoy consuming juicy earthworms. Worms that are living in the wild are usually a much easier target than the domesticated ones that we are dealing with.

Nevertheless you will have to keep an eye out for potential threats and protect your worms from pests to maximize your worm farm's production. So let's see how you can keep the predators away or at least make it as difficult as possible for them to get to your worm-herd.

Birds, toads and frogs
They are easily kept at bay by properly covering your worm bins and beds with lids, plastic sheeting and old carpets. Make sure that the edges of the bed covers are properly secured with bricks, sandbags or something similar.

Centipedes
Centipedes (picture on the right) are dangerous predators who love feeding on worms. They are nocturnal and paralyze their victims with powerful venom before they devour them.

They live on the surface of worm beds and can usually be seen for a few seconds after you have removed the covers. Centipedes are quite fast and will immediately try to hide and run for cover when they feel threatened. If you want to reduce the numbers of predatory centipedes inside your worm beds you will have to destroy them on sight.

When you lift the protective plastic sheet of your worm bed and you see one of the centipedes, quickly grab it between your thumb and index finger and squeeze it. That should be enough to kill it. Then just put it back in the worm bin and the worms will dispose of the remains in due time. Centipedes are usually not a major problem and if you don't feel like killing them and don't mind the loss of some worms, then just leave them be.

Rats
Some rats will eat worms if they can get hold of them. The best way to protect your worms from them is by using rattraps or rat poison.
I prefer a rattrap, as it is a quick death for the rodents. If you deal mainly with horse manure as food and bedding for your worms than the rats shouldn't become a major problem for your worm farm, since they do not seem to be attracted to it. In our many years of worm farming we have had only one rat on the premises, probably transported inside a bag of worm food.

Moles
Moles can become a big problem if they get inside your worm beds. They live more or less exclusively on earthworms and can make serious inroads into your worm-herd if you do not remove them quickly. The best way to avoid losses due to moles is preventing them from entering beds in the first place.

The presence of moles can usually be spotted due to their mounds and surface tunnels which are a sore sight for all gardeners but a good warning sign for every worm farmer. Before you establish a worm bed investigate the surrounding areas for any signs of moles. Take a peak over the fence into your neighbor's plots or ask them if they have had any trouble with moles. If there are no moles in your neighborhood then there will be no immediate danger to your worms.

One good thing about moles is that they are quite territorial and don't get on well with each other. You will usually find that only 1 or 2 moles are responsible for all the damage caused on your worm farm. Once you have caught them the problem should be solved. The exception to their solitary behavior is in the mating season, which is

A worm bed made of second hand bricks.

normally in spring. During that time you might encounter several moles within a small area.

If you want to be certain that no moles can enter your worm beds, it is best to build a bed out of bricks or concrete blocks with a nice strong mesh or a concrete floor at the bottom of the bin. The picture above shows a bulk bed built with bricks. Its works well and protects worms from moles.

The mesh at the bottom has to be fine enough to prevent moles from squeezing through it. Should you not wish to invest in such a solid worm bin at the beginning of your project but fear an attack of moles on your bulk beds, than you must look for other ways to protect your valuable worm herd. If there are moles nearby it would be best to catch them before they find your worm beds.

You should regularly check out the areas around your worm beds and if you see any signs of mole activity, take action to catch and remove the moles immediately.

There are many different types of mole traps on the market from those that catch the moles alive to those that will kill them. If possible I would go for an option that allows you to spare the moles lives but the choice is yours of course.

Have a look on the Internet for suppliers of mole traps, as well as forums that offer solutions and advice on how to build your own traps for basically no cost.

Slugs

These naked snails can be found in many worm bins and some of them are suspected of eating worms. We always remove them. Either place them somewhere else where they will not harm your worms or plants, feed them to your ornamental fish (my Koi fish love them) or destroy them and add them to the compost heap.

Mites

There are 3 types of mites: white, brown and red ones. While the white and brown mites, which are about the size of a pinhead, are not a threat to worms as predators, they do compete with the worms for food. If their numbers increase dramatically this may raise the cost of feeding your worms. We have not had this problem yet and really do not have too many white and brown mites around in our worm beds. So we usually let them be. The mite that is the biggest threat to worms is the red mite. It is a predator and can attack and kill worms by virtually sucking them dry.

But so far we have never had to deal with them in our worm beds. The white and brown mites that multiply sporadically are usually seen in our fattening bins that are almost exclusively fed with dog poop. The mites are attracted to a very moist environment and the abundance of fermenting feed that lowers the pH in the bin.

Ways to prevent mites from entering a worm bin
- Keeping low moisture levels inside the bin.
- Add controlled amounts of food to the bins i.e.: no overfeeding! If a worm farm becomes smelly it is not well balanced and probably contains too much food.
- Limit the amounts of watermelon or other very wet foods used in the worm bin.
- Scatter small amounts of agricultural lime (Calcium carbonate) over the surface of a worm bin to adjust the pH level of the bedding. This will counteract an increase in acidity and establish a neutral pH level in the bin.

Ways to remove mites
There are a few ways to reduce the mite population in your bin. But remember that regardless of the method you choose to use, if you don't change the conditions that attracted the mites to your worm bin in the first place you can be sure that a new army of mites will soon colonize it.

- Cover the surface of an infested worm bed with soaked newspapers. After 24 hours lots of mites will have attached themselves to the newspaper. Remove the newspaper with the mites. Repeat this until the amount of mites in the bin has been reduced significantly.

- Add big pieces of watermelon rind or any other sweetish fruit to the worm bin and leave for 24 hours. Then remove the fruit with the mites that have colonized them. Repeat until you have achieved the intended reduction of mites.
- Expose the surface of the bed to strong light or sunlight for a minimum of 5 minutes. The worms will dig down deeper into

the bedding. Then use a blowtorch or heat gun to kill the mites on the surface of the bed. Repeat until you achieve the intended reduction of mites.

PESTS

These are creatures that will live in or invade a worm bin. Although they do not pose any direct threat to the worms, they can change the conditions of the worm farm in a way that might harm worms in the long run and cause you additional work.

Mice

They are not known to feed on worms but rather on grains. Mice nevertheless might cause a problem as they can quickly multiply and might get out of hand. Occasionally we have had mice on our worm farm but have always managed to contain them quickly. If you want to catch them alive in traps, I encourage you to do so. We haven't had much success with this method. Alternatively you can employ the services of a cat or even a number of cats but I don't like the way cats prolong the suffering of mice before they finally kill them. In most cases we made use of mousetraps, which worked quite effectively after a little trial and error. As bait we use a sunflower seed that we attach firmly to the trap and cover it all around with sticky peanut butter.

It is important to make it difficult for the mice to get hold of the last bit of the peanut butter otherwise they will just strip the trap of the bait without setting it off.

You will have to be patient and employ several traps at once. After you have caught the first one, set up the trap again and place it in the same spot as before. It is most important to catch the big ones, which are obviously of breeding age, otherwise they will continue to produce offspring. If you haven't caught any mice for a couple of days and the traps haven't been stripped of the bait, then the area should be clear of mice. Keep an eye open for golf ball sized holes on the surface of your worm beds. These could possibly been made by mice that are nesting in the lower layers of the bedding. When you have found a regular supplier of horse manure or other manures that are mixed with straw, be careful when you collect the material from the farm or horse stable. The manure and horse droppings are usually packaged in big woven bags. Keep an eye open for bags with small round holes that would be big enough for a mouse or rat to get inside. If you can, stay away from those bags and leave them behind.

As a rule of thumb, for every mouse you see, there are probably between 5 to 10 more around.

Ants

Ants usually don't attack worms but can and will compete with them for food and deplete the worm bed of sugars and fats. If the ants bother you, then you can remove them using a blowtorch or heat gun in the same way you used it to kill mites. Although we regularly find ant colonies in our worm beds we never see them as enough of a threat to attack them guns blazing! So if we find a colony in our beds that affects regular maintenance, we usually use a hand broom and a scoop to sweep them up from below the covers. Alternatively, give the bed a heavy dose of water, which ants really dislike.

Soldier Fly / Maggots

There are apparently more than 1000 soldier fly species globally, and they vary in color from black to green, blue or grey.
They resemble wasps in appearance, which obviously scares away predators. The flies themselves are harmless and do not present a problem to human beings or worms, unlike their maggots / larvae. The maggots are very aggressive feeders and recyclers of organic waste. They can occasionally be found close to the surface of a bin huddling together and devouring food that was intended for the worms.

The maggots of the black soldier fly are used by many people for recycling purposes in a similar fashion to compost worms. However, to my knowledge they cannot be used in the same bins as worms. Black soldier fly (BSF) maggots can however be used to recycle organic waste, on their own, in a separate bin. (This is an interesting subject for another book.)

If BSF maggots become active inside a worm bin, the worms will flee to the lower parts of the bedding, which in most worm bins will be depleted of food. This can often lead to the starvation and death of the worms inside the bin. The bin will start to develop an uncharacteristic bad odor and the bedding will look soggy. If you find BSF maggots in your worm bin you have to remove them as soon as possible.

The best way to do this is to quickly grab them with as little as possible of the surrounding bedding and place them in a bucket or tray with elevated walls. You can then move them to a compost heap or a different bin of organic waste to let them recycle it. Alternatively, remove most of the bedding and worm food they are hiding under, and let them either dry out in the sun or drown them with a little water added to the tray. Once they are dead you can return them to the worm bin. The worms will enjoy them as a high protein food source. You can also use the maggots for fishing or feed them to chickens - if you have any.

Fruit flies
As their name states these flies are attracted by fruit. From time to time they can be found around compost heaps and worm bins. Although they are essentially not harmful to worms, fruit flies can become a nuisance if they are allowed to multiply rapidly. Fruit flies can be identified by their plumb bodies, slow flight and pale brown or orange color.

Mature fruit flies lay their eggs on the peels of fruit, especially bananas. Their eggs are too small to be recognized by the human eye. When the conditions are right (warm and humid) the flies hatch and can quickly multiply in a favorable environment.

There are 2 ways to reduce or eliminate the fruit fly population in your worm bin. Place all your fruit peels and rotting fruit that you want to add to the worm bin overnight in the freezer before you put them into your worm bin. This will kill all fruit fly larvae and eggs that are on the fruit and peels.

Alternatively, build a low cost fruit fly trap. Follow the simple instructions below to produce effective fruit fly traps.

- Take a large empty plastic soda bottle, cut off the top of the bottle at the shoulder where the curve straightens out.

- Throw a few banana skins into the bottom of the empty bottle. With a sharp nail punch 5 or 6 holes of 2 - 3mm in diameter in the sidewalls about 10cm above the bottom of the bottle.

- Place the cut off top piece upside down in the opening at the top of the bottle base. It should look like a funnel now, facing neck down into the cylindrical form of the bottle base. Make sure that it fits tightly and no gaps are left open.

61

- Attach the funnel top to the bottle base with some clear sticky tape.
- Place the trap a few meters away from the worm farm on an elevated spot. If you want to see the building instructions for this fruit fly and gnat trap with helpful pictures go to **www.worm-composting-help.com/fruit-flies.html** and follow the instructions there.

A fruit fly trap in action

It's that easy! You can prepare a few traps with slight modifications to the fruit used as bait, and place them in different locations to find out which works best. Once you have finished your fruit fly traps, open the lid of the worm farm and chase out as many of the fruit flies as you can before you close the worm bin again. The flies, which have an excellent sense of smell, will be attracted by the banana skins to the traps and crawl into the small holes on the side or the funnel opening at the top. Most of them will not find their way out again. You should catch most of the fruit flies that were inside your worm bin within 48 hours.

Once your traps are full, either release the flies somewhere else or wait till they are dead and feed them to your worms. If there are still more flies present, set up the traps again until you have caught all of them.

Fungus gnats
These are also members of the fly family and are similar in size and appearance to a mosquito. They have a slender black body, which easily distinguishes them from fruit flies. Gnats are attracted by

fungi and moisture and can be found in and around compost heaps and worm bins. If you want to reduce the number of gnats in your worm bins, try to reduce the amount of food or reduce the moisture levels on the surface area of your bins. But be mindful of how you do this, as worms need a moist environment to live in. Alternatively, set up some fruit fly and gnat traps to reduce the amount of gnats in and around your worm-bins. We never really have a major problem with gnats and generally just ignore them.

Flies and Fly larvae
In summer it can occasionally happen that flies will lay their eggs on food waste, manure or other animal waste in your worm farm.

Remember that under the right conditions flies will multiply rapidly. There are a few steps you can take to make sure you greatly reduce the fly population in and around your worm beds. One effective way I mentioned previously is to always cover your worm beds and bins properly. If the flies cannot lay their eggs they cannot multiply. When adding food that might attract flies, dig a small trench into your bulk bed, place the food into the trench and cover with at least 10cm of processed bedding or pure worm castings.

In doing so your bed will attract fewer flies and it will be much more difficult for them to reach the food. Whenever you find fly maggots / larvae in your worm bins or bulk beds, immediately remove as many of them as you can. Place them in a bucket and pour boiling water over them. This will instantly kill them. Once the water has cooled down, feed the maggots to your worms.

If you have a surplus of flies on your worm farm and you want to reduce the numbers quickly and keep them away from your home, you can set up a number of flytraps. You build them the same way as the fruit fly traps. However, instead of using banana skins use a little dog poop or fresh manure and add about 5cm of water. There must be no place left for the flies to sit safely without drowning. Shake the flytrap a little and place several of them around the worm bins and bulk beds, ideally in the sun. The flies that are already at your farm will be attracted to the traps and once they have entered the traps most of them will fall into the water, sooner or later, and drown.

Once a trap gets filled with a considerable number of dead flies it will attract even more flies. We found that larger 5 liter bottles work better than the smaller ones. Once you've got the fly population reduced to a more tolerable level, throw the flytraps away or they will attract more flies from the neighborhood. There are some other creatures that you might find inside your worm bins. But the ones mentioned above are the most common ones.

Other residents of your worm farm

Woodlice / Sow bugs
They actually pose no threat to your worms. They are often found in worm bins where they roam around taking their share of the decomposing matter. Worms are not negatively affected by them and both creatures live harmoniously side-
by-side. If you want to remove them either collect them on sight or apply the blowtorch method as discussed earlier on.

Geckos

In some parts of the world you will find geckos in your worm bin from time to time. They are no threat to your worms, preferring to hunt for fruit flies and other small insects. We usually leave them alone.

Springtails

These tiny white insects are part of the recycling process and large numbers of them can be found in most worm bins. They

Tiny white springtails on the surface of a bin

pose no threat to your worms and its best to just let them do their part to convert organic waste into valuable soil conditioner.

Millipedes

Unlike the predatory centipedes, these cute creatures are not predators but rather enjoy consuming decomposing organic materials. Millipedes

A rolled up millipede

are helpful friends inside the worm bin.

TROUBLESHOOTING

WHEN WORMS WANT TO ESCAPE

Acidic bedding will drive worms to escape

A lot has been written about worms and acidity. Acidity is measured in pH and the scale ranks from pH 1 (extremely acidic) to pH 12 (extremely alkaline), with pH 7 being regarded as neutral.

Worms enjoy their bedding most at a pH level of 7 or slightly lower, but can tolerate pH levels from about 6 to 8.5.

Worms quite readily feed on acidic food like fresh manure, animal droppings or citrus fruit peels, but they cannot live in bedding that is acidic. This is why safe bedding is so vital for every worm bin and bulk bed. The safe bedding can serve as a food source, but its main purpose is to provide a comfortable home for the worm-herd to retreat to after they have taken the food on offer.

So although it has often been said that worms are not supposed to be fed with acidic fruit waste, it is not entirely true. The mistake that many people make, especially beginners, is to add acidic food over the whole surface area of their worm bin and then pour lots of water over the surface to adjust the moisture level. In doing so they often turn the whole worm bin into an acidic environment, which will force worms to either crawl to safety or die.

To prevent this from happening it is advisable never to cover a worm bin or bulk bed surface completely with food.

Covering only half of the surface will give the worms a safe retreat should something be wrong with the fresh food that has been added to their worm bin. Another important point is always to soak and drain the manure before you add it to the worm bin. Adhering to these two rules can go a long way to protecting your worm-herd.

Another reason for a buildup of acidity in worm bins is a sudden surplus of food. If you work with manures, grain feeds or dog poop, rather feed regularly and in layers of about 5cm only. This will be sufficient for your worms and will keep them going for a few weeks.

A clear sign of a problem in your worm bin is the presence of many worms above the surface of the bedding and food, clinging to the sides of the bin or the lid and trying to escape.

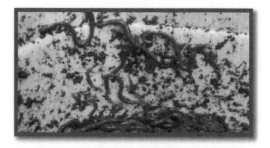

This situation requires immediate action! Quickly remove all the worms that you see from the worm bin and place them in a bin with safe

Worms on the wall of a worm bin are usually a warning sign that the conditions inside the bedding are unpleasant

bedding. If they cling together in lumps remember to carefully separate the worms from each other. If there is an excess of food remove as much of it as you can and place it in another bin that needs food. If the bedding is very wet take all the bedding and food out of the bin and divide it into piles. Exposing the bedding to fresh air will help to get rid of some of the moisture. In an emergency, a good way to counteract high acidity levels in the worm food and bedding is to sprinkle agricultural lime (calcium carbonate) lightly over the surface of the piles before returning them to the bin. But do not overdo it! It should be a light peppering of lime that does not cover every inch of the surface. The lime will need some time to raise the pH level.

Adding crushed eggshells to worm bins on a regular basis also helps to balance the pH level of your worm food and bedding. A good tool to have is a pH meter, which you can push into the food and bedding of your worm bins. This will help you monitor the pH levels. You should find a simple pH meter at one of your local garden centers and they are usually very affordable.

Overcrowded worm bins will drive worms to escape
A naturally grown population of worms in any worm bin or bed will never really have an overcrowding problem. The worms will eat, grow and multiply up to a certain level according to the size of their worm bin or bed, the food supply, and the general environmental conditions. When they feel crowded some of them might crawl off to find a new home. If this is not possible, they will slow down breeding to keep a healthy balance in their living space. The loss of a few migrating worms is normally not really serious because the few worms that left will soon be replaced by newly bred worms.

On a well-run commercial worm farm this overcrowding problem doesn't usually arise because all the breeder bins and bulk beds will receive regular attention and the worm population in the beds is regularly reduced as worms get sold. However, should you feel that a particular worm bed is overcrowded, you can do one of two things: Either harvest some of the worms from the worm bed and add them to another worm bed that is less populated, or harvest some worms from it and start a new worm bed or breeder bin with them.

A point to be considered is that *Eisenia fetida* worms are top feeders and usually live in the upper layers of their living space. When you lift up the cover of a worm bin you should find some worms right beneath it and most of the worm population will be in the top 10 - 15cm of the bin. This means that worms regulate their population in accordance with the surface area of their worm bed rather than the depth of it. We estimate that 1m² of worm bin or bulk bed surface can support 10000 to 12000 worms for an extended period of time, if the appropriate environmental conditions are maintained. This number is only a guideline and depending on your circumstances, the worm population can vary. Keep this in mind when you prepare worms for sale. Your sales container cannot take an unlimited amount of worms. I will elaborate on this in the chapter where I discuss the different products you could offer your customers.

Worms migrate in wet weather

Although the rainy season is a blessing and essential for our survival on the earth it can become a problem for worm farmers. Whereas humans value a home and a dry place away from the rain when a cold front approaches, worms often choose this time to leave their worm bins and bulk beds. They crawl up the walls of

A worm on a wall after a rainstorm

houses, along the sidewalks or into other places around the garden. It is this behavior that represents a danger to them. Often, we have seen hundreds of worms stranded on the street once the morning sun hits the ground and dries up the rain. Others drown in swimming pools, or get washed away in the storm water drains.

It takes just a few minutes for a worm to die once exposed to the sunlight with no place to hide.

In heavy rains, a once thriving worm bin can lose thousands of worms. I've come across several explanations as to why mature worms migrate during wet weather conditions. Many people in the worm farming community believe that there are three possible reasons why worms do this:

69

- Firstly: Worms can drown if their burrows or worm bins get flooded with water that has a low oxygen content. However this shouldn't be a problem for worms in properly constructed worm bins or bulk beds as they are covered and thus little or no rainwater will enter their homes.

- Secondly: Some worm farmers believe that worms can apprehend the wet conditions outside their living space and use this opportunity to move to greener pastures and to new breeding mates. This might be especially true if a worm bin has a high population and the worms feel crowded.

- The third possible reason for their migration is that worms dislike the vibrations that are caused by raindrops falling onto the lids and sides of their worm bins. This theory is supported by the fact that worm bins standing in sheltered places like a garden shed or garage, lose significantly fewer worms than those that are placed in unsheltered areas.

But knowing that many keen worm bin owners do not have the luxury of garages or garden sheds, what are the options for protecting our wriggling friends?

I found a cheap and effective way of minimizing the loss of worms. When we expect rain, we set up what we call "worm shelters" before the wet weather hits our area!

They are actually quite easy to make and fun to work with. What you will need are some old newspapers or cardboard boxes. All you have to do to protect your worms is to place old newspaper (several sheets at once) or flat pieces of corrugated cardboard (the bigger the better) on the ground underneath your worm bins, next to your bulk beds or as close as possible to them.

We use corrugated cardboard because it works best. The cardboard sheets will soak up water in the rain and will offer the escaping worms a place of food and shelter once the sun comes up the next morning.

Worms found under cardboard after a rainstorm

All you have to do then, after a heavy downpour, is lift the cardboard or newspaper, pick up the worms and return them to the worm bin. You can use a soft hand broom and a dustpan to sweep them up or you can take the whole sheet of cardboard and throw it into the worm bin. The worms will love it.

Have a look around and pick up a few bricks or buckets that might have some moisture preserved underneath. Basically anything that can give worms shelter from the rising sun might harbor some stranded worms. You will be surprised at how many worms you may find underneath your worm shelters in the morning after a heavy downpour.

"We found 962 worms after a serious rainstorm, under a single cardboard worm shelter!"

So make use of them. They can save your worms and save you money.

WORM CASTINGS

Worm castings, also known as vermicast or worm humus is probably one of the best organic fertilizers and soil conditioners known to man. 'Worm castings' is actually just a fancy name for worm poop or feces. Your worms should produce a good quantity of this on a daily basis. As worms move through the worm bin they consume large quantities of organic matter (up to half their body weight per day) and deposit it on the surface of their bedding as worm castings.

As worms digest their food they enrich it greatly with calcium, magnesium, phosphates and nitrogen. In addition, worm castings contain up to 20 times more beneficial microorganisms than the organic matter they consume.

Worm castings are water-soluble and release their nutrients slowly to plants as needed. Castings will improve the water holding capacity of soil and will never burn plants. They improve the soil structure and their nutrients are immediately available to surrounding plants. We had spectacular results when growing fruit and vegetables in soil consisting of 80% sand and just 20% worm castings. For example, among the bumper crop of fruit and vegetables were:

- One single tomato plant that bore more than 500 tomatoes over a period of 3 months and

- Swiss chard plants that grew up to 50cm high and yielded beautiful tasty leaves for more than 4 months.

Worm castings have a crumbly structure and are dark in color, which is one of the reasons why they are quite often called "Black Gold." You can mix worm castings with other soil conditioning products like compost or kelp to produce additional products for gardeners and nurseries. Do some research on the Internet and you will find some useful recipes for soil conditioners.

Swiss chard grown in sand and worm castings

How to harvest worm castings
Worm castings are usually harvested once or twice a year from bulk beds. The bulk bed should be filled to a height of at least ½m before you consider harvesting your castings.

About a month before you wish to harvest, stop feeding the bed, monitor for correct moisture levels and let the worms in the bed completely consume the remaining food in the bed.

3 to 4 days before the planned harvest add a layer of fresh food on the surface of the bulk bed and cover it again. The hungry worms will soon move to the new food. By harvesting day, the majority will be close to the surface of their bed.
On harvesting day, early in the morning (6 - 9am), remove all the remaining food from the top of the bulk bed with an additional layer of about 15cm of worm castings. Place all of this in buckets or

other suitable containers. This layer of food and castings should contain most of the herd of worms from the bulk bed.

Now you can freely harvest the rest of the processed castings from the bulk bed. Fill it into buckets with a shovel or spade and strain the contents through a frame of chicken mesh or a similar wire mesh and remove all leftover worms and unwanted material like stones, plastic, weeds and unprocessed food. The mesh size should ideally be between 0.5 - 2. 5cm.

Harvesting castings from small bins can be done in the same way.
Either store the pure worm castings in large bags until you process them or package them straight away into clear labeled plastic bags for sale.

Castings in a bin ready for harvesting

I will elaborate on the bag sizes and labeling, when preparing your product for sale, in a different chapter of this book.

WORM TEA

Worm tea is essentially liquidized vermicast that has been mixed with water and molasses and brewed in an oxygen rich environment.

The brewing process multiplies the beneficial microorganisms and nutrients that are in the worm castings and makes a fantastic liquid plant food and natural fungicide and pesticide.
Worm tea will achieve the best results if used within 24 hours of completing the brewing process but will still be beneficial for several months. If you bottle it just shake the bottle before using it to reactivate the remaining microorganisms.

Like worm castings, worm tea has many positive properties for soil and plants:
- It functions as a natural fungicide and insecticide when sprayed on both sides of the leaves of plants
- When used to water plants, it will act as plant food which will result in better plant and fruit growth
- It will not burn plants
- It will improve soil structure and plant health

It's really easy to produce worm tea and the results will speak for themselves and should satisfy many happy customers.

A simple worm tea recipe
The recipe is worked out for 20 liters. To brew worm tea you need:
- A bucket or tank
- An air pump with some piping
- An air stone usually used for fish tanks
- Some worm castings
- Molasses as food for the microorganisms in the worm castings

- Chlorine free water

When you have all the necessary items together proceed as follows:

- Fill your bucket with water that is chlorine free. If you don't have access to pond water, place an air stone in a bucket of tap water, switch on the air pump for 12 hours and let the chorine evaporate.

- Add 1kg of pure worm castings.
- Add 25 ml of molasses (see picture)

- Let the air pump run for another 24 hours before you remove the air stone.

"You can use the worm tea immediately!"

Should you wish to use the tea as a foliar spray, it is advisable to filter the worm tea through a cloth or a tea strainer to remove any solids

Worm tea filtered through a cloth

that might block the spray mechanism of your bottle. Although properly prepared worm tea can be used pure, it is quite acceptable to dilute it with chlorine free water. A ratio of 5 parts water to 1 part worm tea will still yield great results.

POTENTIAL MARKETS

Now that you've done all the groundwork let's get to one of the most rewarding aspects of starting your own worm business. Money!

Let's explore some of the potential markets you can enter to turn your efforts into income. There are a really wide variety of opportunities available. Although the list below is by no means exhaustive, they are among the more promising and popular options used by worm farmers.

Wholesale and retail

Worms for:

Nurseries	Gardeners
Landscapers	Composting
Worm bins	Breeding stock
Pet shops	Zoos
Bird food	Reptiles
Fish	Fishing clubs
Bait	

Worm farms for:

Nurseries	Households
Hotels	Restaurants
Guest houses	Old age homes
Corporate kitchens	Municipalities
Property developers	Schools

Worm casting fertilizer mixes for:

Nurseries	Landscapers

Worm castings for:

Nurseries	Gardeners
Farmers	Property managers

Worm tea for:

Nurseries	Landscapers
Gardeners	Property managers

Worm tea brewing kits for:

Nurseries	Gardeners
Organic waste collecting services	Private households
Restaurants	Hotels

I trust this gives you some ideas. There are so many possibilities that even the most experienced worm farmers haven't utilized all of them and I am sure that you might be able to come up with new and exciting niches that would suit your local market!

Different markets appear to be prominent in different parts of the world. A hot and dry country like South Africa has limited lakes and rivers and thus a much smaller freshwater fishing bait market than countries such as Germany, U.S.A., Norway or Canada which are known for their numerous rivers, dams and lakes filled with tasty freshwater fish.

On the other hand, South Africa might have a huge market for worm bins and soil conditioners that can improve the amount of fertile soil in the country's gardens and farms. In Australia and South Africa vermicast has been used to rehabilitate salinified soil.

Let's have a look at some of the most promising and profitable markets for your worm business.

Worms for bait (Freshwater fishing)

With millions of recreational freshwater fishermen active all over the world, there will always be the need for live bait. And the

earthworm is by far the most common and desired live bait on our planet. Despite all the artificial lures, the ever growing art of fly fishing, dough's, breadcrumbs, sweet corn kernels and countless secret bait recipes, there will always be a demand for some juicy earthworms in a fisherman's tackle box.

A carp caught with a worm

As discussed previously, bait sized worms require a special diet and will fetch premium prices. They are usually handpicked and packed in small containers holding 25, 50 or 100 worms at a time. It will be worth your while to market to private fishermen as well as tackle shops and fishing clubs, which might purchase bait worms in bulk from you.

Another product you can offer to the eager fisherman is powdered dried worms. This product can be added to other baits to tempt hungry fish to take a bite. It can also be used as food for small fish in fish tanks or as high protein food for fish fry.

This product should be packaged in small attractive bottles or bags and should be offered at a much higher price than live worms.

Worms for domestic worm bins

Taking into consideration that worm farming is still a young industry with enormous all over the world.

More and more people are becoming environmentally conscious and want to assist in reducing the amount of organic waste that is sent to our landfill sites. Worm farms are a good method of achieving this goal. Millions of gardeners are keen to improve the fertility of their soil

A Mini tower worm farm in action

and are eager to either replace the traditional compost heap or add worm composting to their soil conditioning and organic recycling practices.

The number of flat dwellers or those living in apartments using small indoor worm bins is increasing. All those worm bins will need to be stocked with a decent starter batch (at least 500) of composting worms.

Wholesale worms for recycling projects

More and more corporate clients will look to improve their carbon footprint and to reduce the waste they send to landfills.

This is a potentially huge market that has thus far barely been explored. Corporate kitchens, restaurants, hotels and food processing plants produce large quantities of wet waste.

Traditionally this organic waste is collected by contractors and dumped in landfill sites, a very unsatisfactory way to deal with nutrient rich organic materials. The organic matter that gets dumped on landfill sites is just wasted as a potential resource.

In addition, there are direct negative effects produced in the landfills. Most organic matter that gets dumped in landfill sites will decompose anaerobically, giving off methane gas and CO^2, which contributes to global warming. Another consequence of wet waste in landfills is the fact that the rotting matter can pollute groundwater. It is also usually much more costly to dump organic waste in landfills than to recycle it on site.

Recycling kitchen and wet production waste on site with the help of worms can:

- Save the above mentioned industries loads and loads of money
- Convert wet waste into nutrient rich soil conditioners
- Reduce the load on landfill sites
- Assist in the fight against global warming
- Help avoid pollution of ground water

The benefits far outweigh the initial investment and should convince more and more businesses to use worms to recycle their wet waste.

Think outside the box and I am sure you can come up with ideas to introduce this fantastic concept to other potential clients. Schools, hospitals, kindergartens, fruit and vegetable markets and grocery stores are just a few that come to mind.

Worms for breeding stock

More and more people are becoming interested in vermiculture and its products and you might get quite a lot of inquiries from people looking for breeding stock who want to use worms commercially. Amongst those are farmers who will need vast amounts of worms for producing worm castings for their own use. Others will look for breeding stock to start their own worm businesses. Do not worry about possible competitors; you will come across them sooner or later. Fortunately much more worms are needed worldwide than are currently being produced!

81

If you get an inquiry from a potential competitor, sell him the worms. If you don't, somebody else will get his business!

Worm bins for commercial use

This concept goes hand in hand with the previous one and is also a potentially great source of income. When you sell worms in bulk to landscapers, gardeners, nurseries or farmers they might want to use or build their own bins. However, many of them might want to use your bins and your advice to develop a proper set up.

A stackable worm farm, ideal for holding in excess of 27000 worms, and processing an average of 4kg of organic waste per day. That is nearly 1.5 tons annually

Their motivation for farming worms and producing their own castings is that they usually need enormous quantities of soil conditioners. To achieve this they will need bulk quantities of worms as breeding stock, and these worms will need a lot of worm-bin space. You can either supply your clients with plans for bulk beds (described in a previous chapter), or supply them with a sufficient amount of smaller units that can be handled and maintained by one or two people.

The number of bins a client will need depends on the surface area of the bins you choose and the quantity of organic waste they produce. Work on a maximum stocking density of 10000 to 12000 worms per square meter and an average daily food consumption of about 500g for 4000 worms. With this information you can calculate the number of bins they will need to recycle their waste.

This market is enormous and if you can service it successfully, you should do very well for yourself and the environment!

Worms as pet food

Worms as pet-food is another market with huge growth potential. Billions are spent on feed for pets annually, and worms are the preferred food for many kinds of pets.

Ornamental fish in tanks or ponds, snakes, frogs, toads and birds are among the more common animals that find juicy worms irresistible. We have sold worms to pet owners who wanted to improve their pet's diet. Clients that buy worms from us to feed their pets are breeders or keepers of birds, exotic toads, lizards, rats, monkeys, koi fish, goldfish and tropical fish. Potential wholesale clients are pet shops and zoos.

Worm castings and worm tea

Worm castings and worm tea are perfect products for our times. They harmonize with the movement towards a healthier environment, foods and lifestyle.

Worm castings and worm tea are among the best soil conditioners and plant foods known to man.

The market for worm tea and castings can be approached from different

Bottled worm tea

angles. You can sell the worm castings produced by your worms directly to private clients or to nurseries, farmers, property management companies and landscapers in larger quantities. The same applies, to some extent, to worm tea although the benefits of worm tea for soil and plants are at their best during the first 24 hours after brewing. Worm tea that is stored for a longer period of time will lose a lot of its potency but will still be beneficial.

In addition to using it as plant food and soil conditioner, worm tea can be applied as a natural pesticide when sprayed on to plant leaves. Worm tea brewing kits are another product in this market. They could be attractive to hobby gardeners, eco shops and garden centers. You basically have to source the same items you use to brew your own worm tea and sell them as a worm tea kit.

Selling advertising space on your website

A website is definitely something you should think about. Even if you don't want to set up one straight away, in the long run it is a fantastic tool and opens doors to the whole world for you. A well designed website that gets solid traffic will be attractive to advertisers which will bring you extra income. You can offer companies that are active in related fields, for instance nurseries, landscapers or producers of organic products, advertising space on your website.

- Another source of constant additional income can be Google Ad sense.

This income-generating program allows Google to place adverts from other companies with products that relate to your website's content on your site. Google will pay you for each click on one of the ads on your website. The beauty of it is that once it is set up it will generate income for you automatically and you won't have to bother about it again. If you want to find out more and want to give it a try, go to **www.google.com/adsense**, follow the instructions to apply and sign up. Please keep in mind that your site has to be a website with lots of relevant content to be approved by Google. I will give you some more information regarding websites in the chapter that focuses on marketing your products.

SETTING UP PRODUCTS

Once you have a healthy supply of worms for composting, bait worms, worm castings and worm tea it will be time to package them attractively to entice potential clients to purchase.

I believe it is perfectly fine to sell a batch or two of worms in a used plastic bag to a fisherman or a hobby gardener. After all they are usually too many of those dreaded plastic bags around anyway! They work perfectly well as a temporary place for worms to stay and are a low cost packaging solution.

A bag of worms

But when you are marketing to nurseries, garden centers, landscapers, fishing tackle suppliers or eco shops that want to re-sell your products and you have to make your products look attractive.

 Apart from looking pretty, your packaging also has to be designed to ensure a long shelf life for the product.

Worms do need oxygen to live and although they can survive for a while in an airtight container they will die when the oxygen inside the container is used up.

An excessive amount of worms in a confined space will either lead to many of the worms migrating out of your sales container or the demise of the whole worm population inside.

A bucket with compost worms for sale

Attractively packaged products are great advertising tools for your business. We found that self adhesive labels with a logo, contact details and good information about the product, be it worms, worm tea or worm castings, works very well. Below are examples of our products and their packaging to give you an idea of how to set up your product range.

Worms for garden centers, eco shops and other retailers

This is a nice market and once you have clients it will produce regular income. Most of the customers buying worms at garden centers purchase worms to: start their own worm bin, repopulate it after they lost all their worms, add worms to their garden to improve the soil or add worms to their compost heap.

For all of these purposes the minimum quantity of worms we offer is 500, which we sell in attractive 5 liter buckets. The buckets are made from recycled plastic and can hold that amount of worms quite comfortably for several weeks.

You obviously will have to give wholesale customers a decent discount on your retail prices in order to make it worth their while. The 5l bucket comes with a separate lid and a label. Fill each bucket about ¾ full with moist safe bedding and then add your 500 worms and some food on top. *Do not* cover the whole surface and *do not* add water. The bucket should be nearly full to the top. Drill 6 to 8 holes about 6mm in diameter into the lid for air supply. Clean the bucket and stick on the label.

Worms for starter populations

This is also potentially a regular stream of income. Often people do not want to spend the money for a worm bin and prefer to build their own homemade worm bin.

Worms without bedding will cling together. This is stressful for worms and they should be returned to their bin quickly

These people, as well as customers who have lost their worms due to poor management or other unforeseen causes, make up a good percentage of the worm farming market. They will usually buy at least 500 worms and sometimes even 1000 or 2000.

Selling worms is one of the most profitable streams of income in a worm farming business as the costs of keeping and feeding the worms can be really low, thus giving you a serious profit margin to work with.

Have a look at what your competitors charge for worms before you set your prices. If you believe that you will get future business from private clients by selling the worms in attractive and labeled buckets or containers, then give it a try for a while and see if this will boost your sales. Alternatively, as mentioned before, sell your worms in plastic bags to your private clients.

Note: Do not use clear plastic bags as these might expose worms to sunlight.

Bait worms

Bait worms are mostly sold in smaller quantities than those used for composting. We found the best selling quantities are 25, 50 and 100 worms. For these you obviously do not need a very big container. We use a 500ml bucket for up to 50 worms and a 1 liter bucket for 100 bait sized worms. Worms start to

Display bucket for bait worms

lose weight when they are placed in a small confined space with little food and a lot of other worms around. So it is advisable to harvest them just before you sell them.

Bait sized worms should not be in sales containers for longer than 3 weeks without receiving new food. If you are dealing with a tackle shop that purchases bait worms regularly from you, it is good

practice to replace stock that has not been sold after about 3 weeks. This doesn't really cost you a lot and will keep your client happy in the long run.

The buckets used for the bait worms should also be labeled and have 4 to 6 holes drilled into the lid for aeration.

Worm tea

The most commercial sizes for worm tea bottles have been 500ml

Worm tea in used soda bottles

and 1 liter bottles. We sell plant food and foliar spray in both sizes of bottles.

It is important to add handling and storage information to the labels.

Commercial clients like nurseries or landscapers like to order bigger quantities, sometimes hundreds of liters at a time. It is definitely good practice to prepare big batches just before collection or delivery, to insure the worm tea is as fresh and potent as possible.

For bulk orders good sizes of buckets are 20 liter – 25 liter.

Consider offering your worm tea in new as well as used plastic bottles. The used bottles can usually be picked up at recycling centers for a fraction of the price of new ones and go well with the environmentally friendly idea of worm composting. If you establish a solid market for worm tea in used bottles you can encourage the public to drop their second hand bottles at your premises or pop them into containers you supply to retail outlets.

Worm castings

Worm castings are sold in different forms of packaging ranging from opaque woven bags to clear plastic bags and various bucket sizes. We found that the clear plastic bags worked best for us. They show the beautifully dark nutrient rich castings inside the bag and potential customers can see what they are buying.

A bag of worm castings for sale

Worm castings are a top class product and as such should fetch a better price than composts or synthetic fertilizers.

Unfortunately, this is not always the case at present, due to a lack of education on the part of the consumer. But I hope and believe that over time this will change and worm castings will be shown the appreciation and acknowledgement they deserve in the market place. Nevertheless even now you can achieve really good returns on your investment.

When you are selling to private clients and nurseries, decently sized bags will be 2, 5 and 10 liters. Before you bag your castings remove all unwanted materials like stones, uneaten worm food, plastic, wood, metal and glass pieces.

Staple guns used to close bags

A heat sealer

Large worms that might be in the castings should be picked out as well and returned to your bulk beds. Your clients didn't pay for them and the worms might actually starve to death if they stay for a long period inside a plastic bag without food. The bags can either be closed with staples, which is obviously the more cost effective option in the beginning, or with a heat sealer.

Bags prepared with a heat sealer will look a little neater, but in my opinion the stapled bags will do if your budget does not allow for the purchase of a heat sealer.

We usually prick a few tiny holes in the bags incase some small worms are trapped in the bags or others hatch out of cocoons. This method will allow a little oxygen into the bags so that the worms inside the bag do not suffocate. The few worms thus found in the bag of worm castings will represent a valuable free addition for your clients.

Place printed self-adhesive labels with your logo and product description on the bags.

Worm bins

There are quite a few commercial worm bins on the market that are available worldwide. The most widely distributed ones are the "Worm factory" and "Can o worms." They are specifically designed for worm farming and you can contact the producers of these products to see if they would be prepared to supply to you. However, they might already have agents for their products in your country of residence, and may have granted them a sole mandate for this territory. But this does not mean that you will be stuck.

A variety of commercial worm bins

As I mentioned before, composting worms are not really fussy and it does not take a genius to design and produce a small range of worm bins that appear attractive and can be sold domestically and to the wholesale market.

As a matter of fact you can use designing your own range of worm farms to your advantage. Because you do not have to purchase them from other suppliers you will avoid transport costs and possibly import costs as well.

Having to import worm bins might force you to have higher stock levels than you would have if you could produce your bins locally. You would definitely have to bind more of your capital into making the importing process worth your while.

So it is not a bad strategy to build your own range of worm farms at your workshop or home. In order to produce your own "standard

commercial worm bins" you will need the following tools and
accessories:
- 3 plastic bins of the same size
- 1 lid
- 1 tap
- Self adhesive hook & loop tape (Velcro)
- A jigsaw or a strong pair of scissors
- A power drill
- A hole saw set (the kind that fits on a power drill)
- Drill bits 6mm
- Drill bits 3mm

Most commercial worm bins serve the domestic market and are
made out of plastic. Wherever you can, you should try to use
recycled plastic. It is usually cheaper than virgin plastic and
obviously more environmentally friendly. There are no clear cut
rules about the sizes of worm bins but there are two points you
should consider when you go out to source potential bins that you
want to convert into commercial worm farms.

- The bins should be able to service the organic waste of
  households of different sizes.
- The bins should ideally be small enough to be handled by a
  single woman. Female customers constitute a huge number
  of the purchasers of worm bins. So you obviously want to
  offer them a product that they can maintain on their own if
  they need to.

Remember that a worm-bin full of worm castings will hold a lot of
moisture and is usually far heavier than people anticipate. (Imagine
the bin full of wet sand and you'll get an idea).
No two households produce the same amount or type of wet waste
and therefore it's difficult to determine the exact size of worm
farm and number of worms your customers will need. A single

person living in a flat will obviously produce much less waste than a family of 5, especially when waste from a garden and pets are added.

So people are often unsure what size of worm farm they should purchase. It would be a good practice to ask potential clients to weigh their wet waste for one week. If you know the amount of waste they produce it will give you a better idea of the size of worm bin they need. This is common practice when dealing with corporate clients that produce large amounts of waste daily, but it is quite different when you are dealing with private clients who just want to do something for the environment and improve their garden soil at home. They usually want the worm bin straight away and expect you to tell them which size would suit them.

In order to assist them, there are a few guidelines that will help you pick the right kind of bins from your range. Firstly and most importantly, the bins that you choose must have the ability to be stacked on top of each other or, like the "Worm Factory," nestle inside each other (see nestling bins in glossary). This is absolutely vital for multi-tier worm farms

Their ability to stack will ensure that the worms can move upwards from one bin into the next and will also ensure proper drainage to prevent the worms from drowning.

It will also offer the option of adding bins to the worm farm which allows more flexibility for clients to upgrade their system from the standard 3 tier system to a 4, 5 or even 7 tier system, as and when their needs change.

Bins that nestle inside each other touch the surface of the worm food in the bins below and allow worms to migrate upward easily. In the stackable bins worms migrate up easily when the bins are full. It can take several months to fill a domestic bin. Thus nesting bins allow vermicast to be harvested sooner. The nestling systems are slightly neater than stackable bins, but are not essential for successful worm composting. So if you cannot find nestling bins, stacking bins will do the job as well.

Another point to consider is to choose bins that are durable. Speak to your suppliers and ask them for advice. If they want your business they will help! The sources for bins are companies that sell a wide variety of plastic products either retail or wholesale, plastic container manufacturers and companies that sell second hand plastic containers.

Have a look at your local directory listings. Search the Internet for potential suppliers and contact your local chamber of commerce. Browse your local stores and super stores, which generally have a section with different kinds of plastic containers. You might spot one that you find suitable.

Most bin producers add their names and contact details to their containers. If you find the manufacturer's details on the bin, call them first and check out what price they are prepared to offer you direct. It's worth a try.

You will need to source a maximum of 3 different kinds of suitable bins in different sizes to have enough variety to work with. Offering too many choices quite often confuses potential customers. So it is best to keep the range small.

Your smallest (single) worm bin should have a volume of at least 20 liters. The largest one should not be bigger than 50 liters. If you cannot find 3 different kinds of bins do not worry. As long as you have at least one you will be in business.

Next you have to source a tap that you can attach to the bin so that it can be drained of excess liquid when in use. Plastic wholesalers are a good place to start your research. Other potential suppliers will be producers and traders of irrigation or plumbing supplies.

A range of taps that can be used for worm farms

Find some smaller taps like the ones we use. A diameter of 20mm is sufficient. The tap should come with at least 1 washer and 1 nut to make sure it won't leak once fitted to your worm bin. If you can find bins that come with a lid then this will be an added bonus. Most bins that work as worm farms were originally designed for other purposes and do not come with suitable lids. So you might have to make your own lids.

This is not that difficult at all. A flat plastic sheet 4 - 5mm thick will do the trick. It obviously should be opaque to protect the worms from sunlight. Once again finding the right suppliers should be quite easy. Companies that supply plastic sheeting should have the right product for your needs. They usually offer a cutting and delivery service as well. There are different ways to attach the lid to your worm bins. I will show you the method we use at Global Worming. We attach the lids to the bins with the aid of some self adhesive Velcro (hook and loop tape).

We have used this technique for some of our bins for many years. It works quite well and to the satisfaction of more than 99% of our clients.
We get our Velcro from a company that specializes in providing anything that can close and fasten things. They supply a wide range of self-adhesive hook and loop tapes in different colors and widths. We use tape with a width of 25mm.
Purchase the Velcro only once you have your bins so that you know the width of the area on top of your bins walls. Ideally your tape should have the same width as the top of the walls of your bins.

Build your worm bins

Once you have everything you need it is time to make up your first commercial worm bin.

A worm bin with drainage holes

- Start with the bins that will house the worms. Drill holes of about 6mm into the bottom of two bins. The holes should be about 5cm apart from each other.

If you want to make sure the holes will always be placed in a nice regular pattern you can make a stencil out of plywood that will fit exactly into the bottom of your bin and drill holes that are perfectly placed into it. This stencil can then be used in future to speed up production and ensure neat work.

A bin with a hole for a tap

- Next you must drill a hole into the front side of the third bin. Make sure the hole-saw bit or drill bit you use will be just a tiny bit bigger than the diameter of the tap that you want to attach to the bin. Place the tap as low on the sidewall as you can. But leave enough space so that you can turn the nut of the tap inside the bin to ensure a tight fit. Once you have made the hole attach the tap.

- Now have a look at your lid. If the corners of your bins are rounded it would be best to round off the edges of your

- lid to fit them to the shape of your bins. Place one of the bins upside down on top of the lid (previous picture). With a pen or a pencil mark the edges of the bin on the lid and either saw the marked edges off with a jigsaw or cut them off with a strong pair of scissors.

A finished lid

- Depending on the shape and size of your bins cut either 2 or 4 pieces of Velcro to be fitted onto the corners or the front and back of the 2 bins that will house the worms once the bin is in action. Velcro always comes in two parts: the hook tape and the loop tape. We always attach the hook tape, the rougher and harder one, to the bins. The Velcro pieces should be cut to fit the upper surface of the walls perfectly. Make sure that the surfaces that are going to hold the Velcro are clean and dry before attaching the pieces to the bins. Do not to touch the sticky part of the tape with your fingers as the oil in human skin can reduce the stickiness of the tape.

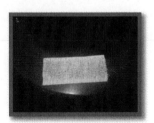

Loop tape attached to a bin

- Place a piece of hook tape on each corner of your worm bin and a piece of loop tape on the corners of the lid. If possible match the color of the tape to the color of your worm bin and lid.
- (In the picture on the previous page I used white tape on a black bin for better visibility). For the lid you will only need half the amount of Velcro that you used for the 2 bins. Cut

- the appropriate amount of loop tape (usually the softer one), remove the paper that covers the adhesive side of the tape and carefully place it with the loops facing down onto the piece of hook tape you attached to the bin earlier.

- Now the sticky side of the loop tape should be facing upwards. Carefully place the lid onto the bin and push down hard to ensure the loop tape gets a good hold on the lid. When you are sure that the loop tape is firmly attached to the lid take it off to test hook & loop connections.

A finished worm farm

There are obviously many different suppliers of self-adhesive Velcro tapes all over the world and they will surely produce a wide variety of Velcro tapes in many different qualities. So you will have to experiment a little to find the perfect sizes of Velcro (hook & loop tape) pieces for your bins. Our bins work with pieces 5 - 8cm in length and 0.5 - 0.8cm wide.

Well done! Your first commercial worm bin is ready for sale!

If you were able to source different sizes of bins, assemble at least one sample of each bin, to see if it's working out the way you anticipated or if there are any unforeseen problems you still might have to solve. If it's not working out exactly the way you had planned the first time, don't worry. Problems are just opportunities in working clothes. You should also test one of each model as a functioning worm bin before you put them on the market. By and large they should work just fine!

Once you have worked with your "commercial" worm bins for some time and there were no problems you will be able to confidently market them to your future customers and need not be afraid of unexpected complaints and comebacks.

Budget worm bins

Although the 3 tier worm bins are the most common type used for worm composting, the "budget" worm bins are another section of the market that you should cover. "Budget" worm bins usually serve 1 to 2 people or those who just are not prepared to invest in a bigger set up.

A 20 liter budget worm farm

I've seen low cost bins that where the size of a shoe box which in my opinion is not a suitable option, as they will fill up way too quickly.

The budget bin we use consists of two 20 liter buckets. The top one which will hold the worms and the worm food nestles inside the other one, which will collect the excess liquid. This worm farm is very easy to produce and much more affordable than larger worm bins.

The buckets should fit comfortably inside each other without getting stuck and there should be enough space left in the bottom bucket to allow for proper drainage of surplus liquids. Should you not be able to source suitable buckets than you can use 2 of the bins that you used for your "standard" worm farms. The important thing to consider is to offer your clients a fully functional worm farm at the lowest possible price.

This type of bin really is gaining in popularity and we noticed that retired people and apartment dwellers go for this option.

In order to produce a budget worm bin you will need the following tools and accessories:

- A power drill
- A hole saw set
- Drill bits 6mm
- Drill bits 3mm
- 2 plastic bins or buckets - minimum volume 20 liters
- 1 lid
- 1 tap

You should be able to find suitable buckets (ideally out of recycled plastic) at the same suppliers from which you sourced your bins. Still, it might be worth your while to contact companies that specialize in the production and sale of buckets. Once you have your buckets and lids prepare them as follows:

- Drill a sufficient number of 6mm drainage holes in the bottom of the top bucket, which will hold the worms. We usually drill 16 holes arranged in a nice pattern. Generally 16 to 25 holes should be fine. To ensure a consistent look and product it's a good idea to prepare a stencil that fits exactly on the bottom of the bucket to guide you while drilling the holes.
We made ours out of plastic, but a stiff piece of cardboard or wooden board will do just as well. To hold the stencil in place we use a few pieces of masking tape to attach the stencil to the bucket before drilling the holes. As most buckets on the market come with airtight lids you have to make sure there

will be sufficient air
supply for the worms
once the worm farm is
in action.

*The bottom of a bin with
drainage holes*

- Use your 6mm drill and
drill at least 6 holes into
the side of the bucket
as high as possible.
They should be placed on opposite sides: 3 on each side.

- Now drill a hole for the tap into the other bucket that will be
at the bottom. Take the same drill bit or hole saw bit you
used for the tap for your "Standard 3 tier" worm bin.

- Once again place the
tap as low on the
sidewall as you can. But
leave enough space to
turn the nut of the tap
inside the bin to ensure
a tight fit. Attach the
tap and test to see that
the connection doesn't leak.

Air holes in the bin

These 2 tier worm bins work quite well and can be used indoors
and outdoors. The handling of the worms, feeding and
maintenance is pretty similar to that of the more common 3 tier
systems. The only difference comes when the bin is full and ready
for harvesting.

You will find the set up and maintenance instructions for the
different worm farms in the chapter titled: *Additional resources.*

You will now be able to produce the following products:

- Buckets with 500 composting worms

- Buckets with 25, 50 and 100 bait worms

- 500ml and 1liter worm tea bottles for use as plant food and foliar spray

- 2, 5 and 10 liter bags of worm castings. The chosen measurement of volume (liters or gallons) is fairer to the customer than a weight measurement, as worm castings can absorb a lot of water and the weight will differ according to the moisture level of the castings

- A range of commercial worm bins

With all the samples you have produced you have a satisfactory range in place to start making you and your products known and raking in some benefits for your hard work!

BUSINESS SENSE

This section includes the following:
- Choosing a business name and developing some promotional material
- Finding out who your competitors are and what products, services and prices they offer
- How to find potential customers
- Entering the market
- Internet marketing with or without a website
- The backbone of a business website
- Interacting with potential customers

Choosing a business name and developing some promotional material

You can have the best products in the world and the fastest and most reliable service anyone can offer but if nobody knows about you and your business, you will not make a single sale!

Once you have your first products ready for sale you can obviously start testing the market and make occasional sales. But before you start marketing on a big scale you should choose a name for your business and create some promotional material.

The basics would be to print some business cards and price lists. When you choose a name for your business pick something that people can remember easily and that you can use for web marketing as well. Once you have the name you have to make sure that it has not been taken already by a competing company.
Do a search on the Internet and call the local chamber of commerce to find out if the name is still available. Choose a name that you can use for your business as well as for a future website. It will help to avoid confusion when people are searching for your

business. Websites like www.domainsbot.com, www.betterwhois.com and www.domaintools.com will help you to make sure your desired business and domain name is still available. If the name of your choice is still up for grabs register it and go to a local printing place that specializes in producing promotional products. Let them help you with a funky logo. Many of those print houses can offer you a full service.

They can help you design your logo, business cards and labels for your products and can laminate and print posters, banners, t-shirts and more.

Do some research about the market and your competitors!

In order to find your place in the market it is important to do some market research first. Who are your competitors, locally and nationally? How much of a market share do they have? Which of their products are competing directly with the items in your product range?

Go to the local eco shops, nurseries, garden centers and garden fairs and have a good look at the products available and the prices and quality of your competitors' products. It is an important task so take your time and do it thoroughly. Your efforts invested here will pay off later. Go onto the Internet and check out your competitors' websites as well.

Find out as much as you can about them.
- What are their products' strengths and weaknesses?
- What prices do they charge?
- Where are their production worm farms and outlets situated?
- Where can you outperform them?
- Can you undercut some of their products' prices?
- Can you offer a better, faster service?

- Do they give enough information about their products?
- What about after-sales support?

Once you've had a good look at this data you should have a preliminary overview of the market situation locally and countrywide. Do your costing to get an idea where you stand and what prices you have to ask for your products to sell them with a profit.

As a new player in the market you might have to undercut the prices of some of your competitors' products or offer a better, faster more personal service. Fast and reliable service goes a long way with clients.

How to find potential customers

When you are getting ready to enter the market and offer your products you will have to know who your future clients will be and what they are looking for. You will be glad to know that people from all walks of life are interested in worms and are keen to acquire a worm farm.

There are plenty of markets for your worm business and lots and lots of potential clients you can approach.

Many people are just environmentally conscious and want to recycle their own kitchen and garden scraps. Others are keen gardeners and want a worm farm to have a regular free supply of worm castings and worm tea for propagating their plants.

There are countless pet lovers who want worms as a staple food or as treats for their animals. Do not forget the millions of fishermen who use worms to catch their favorite fresh water fish. Zoos, schools, hotels, restaurants, farmers, garden centers, gardening clubs, landscapers, animal shelters, dog clubs and hospitals are potential clients for you. The list is endless.

Based on your assessment of the types of market in your city and country, start with the obvious local markets first and then spread out into other areas.

The 3 sectors in most countries that are probably the easiest to penetrate are:

- Private households (that want to recycle their kitchen scraps)
- Garden centers and
- Freshwater fishermen.

Initially, when you set out to market to a certain sector, stay focused to make the most of it.

Private households will either want worms or a complete worm farm. Nurseries and garden centers might be interested in your whole range. Be aware though that no two managers have the same vision. Some are cautious and always order the same small quantities of a limited range of items, others regularly order generously from your whole range. In our experience, the product that appeals to most managers of garden centers is the bucket with 500 composting worms. This offers really good profit margins too. When you contact the manger and get an appointment, make sure that you bring samples of your range to view.

The easiest places to find fishermen that want worms for bait are fishing clubs and pet and tackle shops.

Once you have tried these 3 easier markets, you can choose to move on to other markets that you feel have potential.

Entering the market

There are obviously a lot of ways to make yourself known and spread the word about your products. You can go to eco and garden fairs, craft markets or place adverts in local papers and classifieds.

Another good way to put your business on the map is giving free talks and workshops in garden centers, gardening clubs and schools.
Although you are offering your workshop or talk for free you will raise awareness and you will probably get orders from the audience, their friends and neighbors in the future.

A positive consequence of workshops in nurseries and garden centers is that the manager of the place may be more motivated to stock your products when they see that visitors are keen on the concept of worm farming. The good news is that many people that frequent these places are keen on the idea!
All this effort will help you get a better understanding of your niche market. If you are happy with just a little extra income these steps will be very helpful in getting you started.
But if you want to create a decent income from your worm business, you have to try and obtain more wholesale clients like nurseries, garden centers, and pet and fishing tackle shops. It might be a challenge to get your products listed with some of the local or national retail outlets but once you are in and are providing excellent service at competitive prices, you will receive a steady stream of income from them. Remember that to be a supplier of a retail store, it is important that you look and act professionally and are prepared and well organized.
A manager or buyer of a large garden or wellness center will most probably expect to be provided with all the necessary information in order to make an informed decision whether or not to stock your products. You need to have with you a copy of your price list and

some sample products, which are in perfect condition, professionally packaged and displayed. You should know your production capacities, delivery times and the payment terms that you are prepared to offer.

Bigger stores expect better terms from you. Smaller clients might pay you cash on delivery while larger stores may expect 30 or 60 days credit. It is advisable to first supply smaller shops in order to get a feel for it and to see if you can process orders swiftly and professionally. Once you are confident of your business's production capacities, you can attempt to land some bigger fish on your client list.

Internet marketing with and without website

If you want your business to look professional and want to reach the widest possible audience with very little financial input, you have to make use of the Internet. It is by far the most effective tool available these days.

The Internet is the door to the world and it is absolutely essential to create some sort of web presence for your company and your products.

To get a quick start, you should create some free adverts on classifieds websites. It only takes a few minutes to register and place your adverts. Make sure you add some good pictures of your worm farms and the other products in your range. Advertisements with photos tend to get much better results than those without. Websites offering classifieds services often allow you to swiftly repost your adverts once they have expired. These adverts will potentially give you nationwide exposure. If you have done your homework concerning market research, and your products, services and prices are competitive, they should bring you business.

In the long run though, it is imperative that you set up a website for your business. Your website will be your shop front and you will get visitors from all over the world. There are countless ways to go about creating a website. You must decide which option will be the right one for you. Do you want to go for a free website that companies like "Weebly" or "Yahoo" offer or are you prepared to invest a little more? The free website option might be appealing initially, but I believe that you will face too many disadvantages down the road. One of them will be that you will have to carry your service provider's name in your URL. It will look something like this www.worm-business.weebly.com

A web address like this, which contains the name of your service provider, carries less weight than one with your own domain name. A free website, although perfectly fine to get your name out with very little effort, is somehow associated with being a small player. Even if you are just starting out, it may put you in a category that you do not want to be in.

If you do not know a programming language that you can use to design your own website you will be left with two options for achieving a professional looking website. You can either ask a web development company to create your website for you or you can create one yourself.

The first route will be far more costly than the latter and has quite a few disadvantages. Professional web designers charge a lot of money for their services and you will still have to prepare all the content your site is supposed to have, on your own, anyway! You will have to rely on them to maintain and edit your pages when the need arises. This will add future costs to your business. It may slow you down when you want to quickly place a special offer or adjust prices, since you are dependent on your service provider to implement those changes for you.

We have a website that was created by professional web developers and although they were quite helpful, we clearly noticed that we had to rely on someone else to get our website updated. The website is still active but has not been properly updated in years because the web development company we used went insolvent and other web developers want to charge us big bucks just for a few small changes.

In order to get our site onto the first page of Google we regularly have to run some adverts at "Google Ad works." This brings in orders but is a costly affair.

To save costs and be in charge of our own website, in June 2012 I started with our new website www.worm-composting-help.com.

"I created the entire website myself and in less than 6 months had 33 pages of my site on No. 1 positions on Google. Another 6 months down the line, there were 61 pages occupying the top spot in Google search rankings!"

The traffic we are getting is continuously growing. The new website has totally outperformed our old one which had a head start of many years. Have a look at it and you will see that it looks really good.

The great thing about it is that my service provider charges me less than $1 per day and taught me *everything* I needed to know in order to build a website from scratch! All the technical and Internet related issues that are involved in creating and running a successful website are handled by my service provider. I only have to do what I do best and that is sharing my passion and knowledge about worm farming, the environment and gardening with my audience. Everything else is taken care of for me! It is a turnkey solution and the tools available to me, together with the ongoing support are mindboggling. I was not only informed in detail how to set up a successful website, I also learned how to attract a continuously growing stream of visitors looking for my type of products. Furthermore, I learned how to sell my products, as well as generate new ways of making money through the website. These additional streams of income will continue to flow even if I do not sell worms or worm farms for a while.

Go to my website www.worm-composting-help.com/why-sbi.html and follow the link "SBI a way to personal freedom." Take the time to watch the video. It is free and absolutely worth the effort!

Regardless of which walk of life you are from, with this great system you will be able to give your home-based business an exceptional boost. Everything you need to know; from how to get your website registered to creating an online income, is only a mouse click away! It is explained in such an easy way that even I could understand it ;-)!

The cherry on top is the promise by the service provider to give you your money back if you are unhappy with the hosting, the website or the web business building tools. If you try their product and it is not what you expected, the company promises to refund you up to 3 months after purchase, no questions asked! (These were the conditions in January 2013).

The backbone of a business website

No matter which option you choose, your website should consist of at least 5 pages!

- *Home page*: Gives an overview of your business, vision, goals and mission statement.
- *About Us:* This page should have pictures and background information about you and if applicable, your staff (This page

shows your visitors who you are and is supposed to build trust).

- *Contact*: Gives your clients the option to interact with you. It should contain your physical or postal address, a contact phone number and an e-mail address.
- *Products page*: This is obviously your online shop or show room. It should contain pictures, descriptions and the prices of your range of products.
- *Order Page*: On this form you give your visitors the option to order products online. The page should have fields for your clients to fill in their details and contact information and allow them to order the product of their choice.

These 5 pages should be enough to get your online business off the ground. They are the backbone of an online business website.
But you should not stop there. The more of your knowledge you share with your visitors, the more trust and the better reputation you will build. This will result in more pre-sold visitors and potential customers. So you should keep on adding quality information to your website to attract more visitors and grow your online business.

Interacting with potential customers
Whenever you promote your business, whether through conversation with a potential customer, through pamphlets or on your website, vital for success is that you have a good sales pitch and that you do not come across as too pushy.
Make sure you emphasize all the outstanding benefits that your products will offer.
I have jotted down a few points to consider using in your sales pitch:

Benefits of products

- A **Worm farm** reduces waste that would otherwise go to landfill sites and reduces the production of greenhouse gases, which contribute to global warming. It also produces worm castings and worm tea which are organic fertilizers and natural pesticides.

- **Worm castings** are top quality organic fertilizers and soil conditioners. They will slowly release their nutrients when the plant needs them. A handful of worm castings consists of about 5 billion living organisms and can feed an average potted plant for up to 6 months. Worm castings can never burn plants or their roots and can be used to produce worm tea. Castings will save gardeners and farmers money that they would have spent on expensive fertilizers and will improve the taste of fruit and vegetables grown from worm casting enriched soil.

- **Worm tea** is a fantastic liquid plant food and natural pesticide. It can be used as a foliar spray on leaves or as fertilizer around the base of plants, will never burn plants or roots and can be used in concentrated or diluted form with 5:1 parts of water to worm tea.

- **Compost worms/earthworms** will dig tunnels in the soil that allow more air to penetrate the ground and will condition and fertilize the soil. The worm tunnels can hold water, making it available to the roots of plants.

- **Worms for fishing and pet food** will make excellent bait for freshwater fishing and can be used as high protein food for lizards, monkeys, birds, fish, frogs, rats and many other animals.

This is by no means a complete list, but gives you something to work with.

Free!

Now here is an amazing word that you can use to make sales! An important technique you should consider implementing when promoting your business is to make use of this powerful word! People seem to be magically drawn to products or services they can get for free! It is a bonus that makes any deal sound even more enticing and can be the final straw that will convince your prospective customer to buy. Your free offers do not necessarily have to cost you anything but will still draw many of your clients to purchase from you.

Here are some examples of free products or services you can offer:

- **Free worms** with each purchase of a worm farm. The worms do not really cost you much. Make sure though, that you obtain a decent profit on your worm farms.
- **Free set up and maintenance instructions** for worm farms. This will give clients confidence that they will be able to manage a worm farm and keep the worms alive.
- **Free telephonic after sales service** at any stage. This is another step to encourage wary customers to go through with the purchase. Emphasize that they need not contact you via email but rather call you if they have questions or problems with their worms or worm farms.
  Make sure to **only** offer free *telephonic advice*. This will make it much easier for you to find out what is wrong with your client's worms or worm farms, and how to take corrective steps. Responding to emails might take a lot of your valuable time and you might have to write back and forth several times to establish what is going on in your client's worm farm. Apart from some worms and a little of your time, none of those free offers will really cost you anything, but will go a long way to making your potential customers feel they are getting a good deal for their money and are cared for!

PACKAGING AND DELIVERY

Choosing the right way to send your products
If you supply to local clients who pick up the ordered products from you, you do not have to bother with protective packaging. Just make sure the product is ready for your client when they arrive at your premises and that the product is in excellent condition.

However, for orders that you have to send to other parts of the country either by courier or through the postal service, you have to ensure that the products arrive without being broken.

We usually use the post office to send out our products as they offer us a flat rate to any destination nationally and are in most cases significantly cheaper than commercial courier services.

Another problem one may encounter when using courier services, is the fact that you hardly ever get a flat rate from them and you may have to obtain a new quote for each shipment that goes to a different destination. This causes a problem if you are offering your products on a website, as you will not be able to state how much the courier fee would be.

I suspect that the post office might be the cheaper option in most countries. However, only you will know how reliable your country's postal service is. Using the post office allows us the freedom to give our delivery prices online with our products and order pages, which helps to secure deals with impulse buyers!

Clients like the ordering process to be simple and efficient. The more steps it takes to close the deal the more likely it is that you will lose the sale!

In order to determine which method of delivery works best in your town and country you should investigate both options and see which one is best for you.

We do 90% of our nationwide deliveries through the post office but sometimes clients would prefer to have their worm farms or worms delivered by a courier service. If this is the case we gladly provide a quote from a courier company. Than the ball is in their court and if they are happy with it we go through with the deal.

Preparing your products for post or courier
Making sure your worms arrive alive!

When you send your products up country you will obviously have to ensure that they arrive in one piece and in good condition. At the same time you want to keep the packaging and postage costs as low as possible.
After experimenting with different packaging materials, we settled on using the following for most of our shipments:

- Polystyrene boxes
- Plastic bags
- Pallet wrap
- Packaging tape / cable ties
- Paper packaging (this is only used occasionally)

The products we ship the most are the 3 tier worm farms. They are not very heavy and are relatively robust. When you want to get a 3 tier worm farm ready for transport, you have to make sure that all the parts will be protected from breakage and that the worms will arrive alive. This is not a difficult job and you should have no problems sending your worm farms to the furthest places in your country without incident, unless postage often takes longer than two weeks.

A standard worm farm consists of

- 3 bins
- 1 lid
- 1 tap
- 1 batch of worms

The bins and the lid are quite solid but the worms and the tap need to be specially protected during transport. The worms will need to be protected from extreme temperatures during transport and need to be kept

A polystyrene box with air holes

moist as well. The best way to achieve this is to place them in a polystyrene container filled with safe bedding. The box should fit inside one of the worm farm's containers and should have a volume of at least 5 liters. Punch about 20 holes for oxygen flow into the lid and upper part of the walls of the polystyrene box (see picture). Then place it in the middle bin of the 3 bins of your worm farm. Make sure that the lid will stay in place during transport. We normally just tape 2 sides of the lid down with a piece of packaging tape.

Worms and safe bedding in a polystyrene box

You also have to ensure that the box stays in one place inside the worm farm container. For this purpose you can use cable ties. Depending on the size of your box and the cable ties, you might have to tie 2 or 3 cable ties together. Connect the cable ties through 2 holes in the bottom of the middle bin and then strap them together over the top of the polystyrene box (see the picture)

Because the polystyrene box needs to stay firmly in place the cable ties need to be strapped quite tight. You can place some protective cardboard pieces over the lid of the polystyrene box to prevent damage by the cable ties.

Polystyrene box with cable ties and tap

Whenever possible, we use *"B grade"* or second hand polystyrene boxes as they are obviously available at a lower cost than brand new boxes.

An even cheaper way of packaging the worms for transit is to use used plastic grocery bags and string. You can put the worms and their bedding into the bag and close the top of the bag with 2 loose knots. Fix the bag with the string to the bottom of the worm bin. Make sure to leave a little opening at the top of the bag to allow oxygen into the bag during transport. Only send worms in plastic bags if you are certain that they will not encounter extreme temperatures while in transit!

A Midi tower worm farm ready for transport

Once the box with the worms is tightly secured, attach the loose tap with some sticky tape to the cable ties on top of the worm box. Put the top box with the lid back in place and wrap the worm farm up with the pallet wrap and tape.

Posting worms

When sending worms without a
worm farm, the packaging may
differ. It will depend on the
temperatures outside and the
quantity of worms that you are
shipping. Worms always need to
be packaged with some safe
bedding for travel. As a rule of
thumb add at least 5l of bedding for

***A polystyrene box without air
holes***

every 500 worms in your shipping container.

When sending worms in a period of moderate temperatures of 15 -
25 °C, you can send worms in woven bags, large plastic bags or
cardboard boxes. The cardboard box should be lined with a plastic
sheet.

If you want to avoid any risk of the worms getting overheated or
freezing to death, then send them in an insulated container that
can protect the worms from extreme temperatures.

For this purpose, we use polystyrene boxes that are available in
different sizes. Even large fish like tuna are packaged in such
containers.

As mentioned before, when buying the boxes ask if you can
purchase reject or B grade boxes. Being a relatively soft item the
boxes quite often come with small flaws from the production
process. They will either be sold at a reduced price or crushed and
sent back into production. We try to buy all our boxes from reject
stocks. These boxes are usually in good condition and sometimes
one is unable to even spot the defect! If the box has a small chip
somewhere, that will not bother the worms at all! When you place
your worms in the polystyrene box you have to make sure that

there are some air holes for the journey. Punch a fair amount of holes into the lid and the upper side of the walls. Then add worms and bedding to the box and close it.

Make sure the lid will not come off and then wrap the worms carefully in wrapping paper.

Paper will allow some additional oxygen into the travel container should it be needed, but this is unlikely to happen under normal circumstances.

It is important that you fill up your box with safe bedding to about 80% of its capacity. This will leave some extra space for oxygen in the box and prevents the worms from flying back and forth in a poorly filled box during transport. Do not squeeze the bedding into the box but rather place it gently inside. This way there will be oxygen pockets in the bedding that will further benefit your worms.

Place printed stickers on the box that indicate that the content is fragile. If you are allowed to do so in your country, stickers like "live worms... handle with care" would be a good idea.

When you send worms either by post or courier you do not have to use the overnight service, which is quite expensive. Worms can live quite happily in a properly packaged and handled transport container for 2 to 3 weeks. Use the standard or economy service. They usually take 3 to 7 days and will save you a lot of money.

Note: Not all clients are honest and from time to time you might get an email or a call from a client who insists that all the worms arrived dead!
Rarely is this actually true. I estimate that if the worms are properly packaged and handled, 99% of all worm transports will get the

worms to their destination alive and well. If you are contacted by a client who claims that his worms died during transport ask him why he suspects they are dead. If he says that he only sees a few worms when inspecting the worm bedding then the worms in the box are probably just fine. Worms are usually quite lethargic and are not easily visible if they have been travelling in a box for a while.

If worms die in a box then in most cases they will all die off rapidly. The result will be a terrible odor, which one will notice when the box has been opened!

If the contents of the box do not have a strong odor, the worms should still be fine!

A method that calms down most clients is to kindly ask them to add the worms with the bedding to the worm bin, water them, give them some food and cover them with thick newspaper and a plastic sheet for 2 weeks. Usually after 14 days, the client will find the worms alive and active right beneath the newspaper.

Nevertheless, offer to send them free worms at your own cost, if this is does not happen. If you suspect that the worms have actually died, or the client does not back down, or calls you again after 2 weeks to complain that the worms are not alive, politely offer to send another batch of worms. It does not cost you that much and you will have a satisfied client.

Posting worm castings and worm tea
Both bags with castings and bottled worm tea can be prepared for transport with pallet wrap and paper packaging.

SHOW ME THE MONEY

Choosing the right payment terms

Generally, when dealing with private customers who come to our workshop to purchase a product, we work strictly on a COD (Cash on delivery) basis. This will probably be the same all over the world. A significant part of our worm farming business transactions are done through online orders from people that live hundreds or even thousands of kilometers away.

So how should one deal with those clients? Send them the ordered product and hope they will pay afterwards?

If you are living in Utopia or a place where honesty and integrity are guaranteed, you might be prepared to do business this way. We, however, send our clients an invoice with the order confirmation and politely ask them to transfer the money into our account so that we can process their order. This works really well and we have hardly ever had a potential client that refused to pay before receiving the ordered goods. So, to be on the safe side, stick with the methods of either "PBD" (Pay before delivery) or "COD" (Cash on delivery)!

When dealing with wholesale clients, in many cases the terms will be different as bigger clients expect you to offer them more favorable terms. As I mentioned before, the bigger the client the more they will want to dictate the terms and will probably expect you to grant them 30 days or longer before paying for the stock.

You should do some research before dealing with new wholesale clients and decide how to approach and work with them in accordance with the results of your investigation.

RULES AND PERMITS

Farming with earthworms is generally a very environmentally friendly practice that brings many benefits to individuals, communities and our planet. Nevertheless when one is working with large amounts of decaying organic matter there may be rules and regulations one has to adhere to in order to avoid problems with neighbors or the authorities.

Due to ignorance, some people really believe that worm farming might be harmful to the environment, but to my knowledge I have not heard of a single worm farmer anywhere who has been forced to close his business due to environmental concerns.

Should you encounter a neighbor who voices concern about your worm-farming project, explain to them in a friendly way, the great benefits that your activities offer the environment and future generations. This will usually go a long way to easing their concerns and may even spark the interest of those who have not heard of worm composting before.

Nevertheless each country has its own legislation and it is always advisable to have a look at your local laws concerning the composting and recycling of organic waste. You should find that most municipalities are in fact grateful to anyone who helps reduce the pressure on local landfills.

ADDITIONAL RESOURCES

Although vermicomposting is very easy, most of your customers will expect you to supply them with set up and maintenance instructions for the worm bins they purchase.

Below are basic instruction sheets which you can give to your customers, explaining how to maintain the different kinds of commercial worm bins.

Standard 3 tier worm bin set-up and maintenance instructions

- *Find a place out of direct sunlight for your bin, to prevent it from overheating.*

- *Place a layer of approximately 7cm of moist shredded paper in the bottom of your middle bin.* Shredded paper should be soaked in water for at least 1 hour and then drained.

- *Place the worms, with the bedding they traveled in, on top of the shredded paper and cover the bin with the lid.* Your worms will burrow down and start feeding.

- *Start adding food in small quantities at first; say approximately a cup of food per day for 500 worms.* Place the food on top of the bedding and cover it with a soaked newspaper or a piece of old plastic sheeting. *If all goes well, keep doubling food quantities every two to three months, till the bin reaches capacity. You will recognize this when the food starts to pile up.*

- *The contents of the bin should always be moist.* Worms need a moist environment to breathe. If it gets dry add some water. Avoid fresh tap water because of its chlorine content.

- *Under the right conditions your worms will not leave your bin.*

- *Worms are top feeders and will always migrate upwards to follow the food supply.* Once your middle bin is full start adding food to the bin on top of it. Most of the worms will migrate upwards towards the food.

- *The excess liquid of your worm bin will drain into the bottom bin (the one with the tap),* and can be harvested as worm leachate (liquid plant food).

- *After approximately 4 to 6 months you should be able to harvest your first load of nutrient rich worm castings.*

- *Empty the middle bin and place it on top of your compost system and start filling it again.*

Find more info at: www.worm-composting-help.com.

IMPORTANT NOTICE
- ❖ Each Worm Farm comes with a starter batch of worms
- ❖ Worms are picked from bulk beds and come in different sizes
- ❖ Due to handling and transport, worms might lose weight rapidly and take up to 14 days to become active and feed again

For further maintenance instructions, with illustrations, for multi tier worm farms go to:
www.worm-composting-help.com/worm-farm.html

For further information about worm farms and how to start one, have a look at the following link:
www.worm-composting-help.com/starting-a-worm-farm.html

These pages have been set up by us and are constantly maintained and updated. They also provide opportunities to post your questions or suggestions on any topic related to worm farming.

Budget 2 tier worm bin set-up and maintenance instructions
- *Find a place out of direct sunlight for your bin, to prevent it from overheating. This could be either indoors in a cool area, or outdoors out of sunlight.*

- *Place the worms and their bedding on top of the drain inside the upper bin.*

- *Start adding food in small quantities at first; say approximately a cup of food per day for 500 worms.* Place food on top of the bedding and cover it with a soaked newspaper or a piece of old plastic sheeting. *If all goes well, keep doubling food quantities every two to three months, till the bin reaches capacity. You will recognize this when the food starts to pile up.*

- *The contents of the bin should always be moist.* If it is too dry add some water. Avoid fresh tap water due to its chlorine content.

- *If the conditions in the worm bin are correct, your worms will not leave your bin.*

- *Worms are top feeders and will always migrate upwards towards the food supply.*

- *For the first few weeks, open the lid of your worm bin once a day to check if all is in order.* A healthy worm farm will never develop bad odors.

- *The excess liquid from your worm farm will accumulate in the bottom bin.* The worm tea (liquid plant food) can be harvested by tapping it off.

- *After approximately 4 to 6 months you should be able to harvest your first load of nutrient rich worm castings.*

Harvesting the worm castings and separating them from the worms

- Once the worm bin is full, empty the contents of the worm bin on a table or board outside in the sunshine or under bright lights.

- Gather the contents of the worm bin loosely together into the shape of a cone and wait 10 minutes. The worms in the bedding will crawl towards the center of the cone to avoid the sunlight.

- After waiting the allotted time, scrape off the surface of the cone of worm castings or worm compost until you reach the worms that are hiding from the sun.

- Give the worms another 10 minutes to dig deeper into the soil to escape from the sun and then remove more worm castings until you reach the worms again.

- Repeat these steps until all worm castings are separated from the worms.
- Now quickly place about 10cm of worm castings on top of the drain of your upper worm bin. Place the worms and some food on top of the castings and restart your worm bin.

- Avoid very hot days for doing this work and never leave your worms exposed to the sun for more than 1 minute without some bedding or castings to hide in. Worms die very quickly if they get exposed to sunlight!

INTERESTING FACTS ABOUT WORMS AND THEIR ENVIRONMENT

- Compost worms breathe through their skin.

- They need a moist environment to live in.

- Worm castings are an amazing soil conditioner and plant food.

- A small lump of castings the size of a golf ball consists of about 5 billion living organisms and can feed an average pot plant for up to 6 months.

- 5liters of castings can fertilize about 5m² of topsoil.

- Worm castings release their nutrients to the plants slowly and only when the plants need them.

- Worm castings will never burn plants or their roots.

- Of the thousands of kinds of earthworms only about a few species can be used commercially.

- In captivity, compost worms (*Eisenia fetida*) can eat up to half their body weight in just one day.

- 4000 compost worms weigh abou*t 1kg.*

- *Earthw*orms can be found on all continents except Antarctica.

- Compost worms are hermaphrodites and after mating, both worms will carry fertilized eggs.

- Under ideal conditions compost worms can live for more than 10 years.

- Worms that are torn or cut into two will not survive as two separate worms. Apart from being a cruel practice it will usually kill both halves of the worm. The front part which holds all the vital organs might have a slim chance of survival while the back part will certainly die.

- Worms can live submerged under water for many months as long as the water provides enough food and plenty of oxygen. Otherwise, they will suffocate.

- Worms don't eat fresh organic waste but rather the parts of the organic matter that are starting to decompose.

- A healthy, well-managed worm farm will not produce bad odors no matter what materials are used to feed the worms.

- Many earthworms serve as excellent live bait for freshwater fish.

TO CONCLUDE

Now that you have read and worked through this book I hope that it has inspired you to move forward and start your own worm farming business.

Do not worry if it all sounds overwhelming right now. Rome was not built in a day. All projects in life, no matter how challenging, have started with the first step! In all of us there is the possibility for success.

If you are passionate about worm composting, and want to make some extra income, be your own boss and have only a very small budget for your project, than a worm farming business could be the right solution for you!

For additional assistance you should have a look at the following: www.worm-composting-help.com. My interactive website is constantly updated and is full of information about worm composting and organic gardening. You will find many interesting articles with full color pictures and opportunities to communicate your ideas and questions.

THE AUTHOR

As long as I can remember, I have loved the outdoors and have cared about the environment. I grew up in Germany and moved to South Africa in 1995. In 1998 while working on a Koi farm, I accidently (or so I thought) stumbled upon the subject of worm farming.

We initially raised worms as a high protein food for our Koi fish but as I researched the subject of worm farming (vermiculture), I became totally fascinated by these wriggly creatures and decided to start my own worm farm and promote worm composting.

The Author and his nephew Mika

In 1999 I started one of the pioneering worm farming companies in South Africa - *Global Worming.* I initially started with just 1000 composting worms, which have now been multiplied into millions.

Countless households and businesses have purchased worms, worm farms, worm castings and worm tea from us.

We made a video about the basics of worm farming for the city of Cape Town that can be viewed on our homepage at www.globalworming.co.za and have given seminars about worm composting on behalf of the *Botanical Society of South Africa* and the *Department of Environmental Affairs* of the City of Cape Town.

I believe that the potential of earthworm farming has only just begun to be recognized. In the years ahead, many people around the world will see the huge benefits of worm farming and will implement it.

The low start up costs are especially practical for poorer and disadvantaged communities where there are already some pioneers who use compost worms to recycle their organic waste into nutrient rich worm castings. Worms, worm tea and worm castings can be used to grow nutritious fruit and vegetables in pots, containers, backyards or wherever there is available space.

The worm industry although already a multimillion Dollar/Euro industry, has plenty of room to grow and will be able to support various sizes of worm farming businesses all over the world.

I wish you all the success you are hoping for!

Yours
Stephan Kloppert

GLOSSARY OF TERMS AND TOOLS

Aeration
Worms need oxygen in their environment to live. It is essential that the worm bin has a regular air supply. Just a few openings provided by the gaps between some stackable bins, or three to five air holes of at least 5mm in the walls on opposite sides of the bin, should suffice.

Bedding / Safe bedding
The organic material that worms live in inside the bin or worm bed, which also serves as a retreat in when there are dangerous or harmful conditions in the food layers of the worm bin / bed.

Breeder boxes
Small bins stocked with mature worms that will constantly produce infant worms for the worm business. Never sell worms from your breeder boxes! Breeder boxes are the engine of your business and should never be depleted.

Bricks
Bricks are used to hold down the edges and sides of the plastic sheets and carpets that cover the bulk beds. This helps to keep the moisture level of the feed layer of the bulk beds favorable and acts as a natural barrier against invaders like flies dogs, or birds. Small concrete blocks, stones or boards can obviously be used instead of bricks.

Broom and dustpan
During the daily work with worms and after rainstorms, worms can get stranded, and may die. Scooping them up with a soft brush or broom and returning them to the worm bin can save these worms.

Buckets
20l buckets are used to move large amounts of harvested worms from bulk beds. They are also useful for moving compost, worm castings, worm food and water.
Note: the measurement in liters can be converted into U.S. gallons (standard liquid) using the conversion table at the end of the book.

5l buckets are used to house and sell 500 worms (a good starter population) to private clients and nurseries. 1l buckets are used to measure worm castings and worm teas that are prepared for sale. Adapt these size measures to those roughly similar in size that are readily available in your country.

Carpets
Old or second-hand carpets are very useful as covers for breeder bins and bulk beds. They protect and prolong the lifespan of the plastic covers underneath and act as protection against predators and the sun.

Clitellum
It is a thickened band approximately 1 - 2cm behind the head (segments 14 to17) of a mature worm that is part of the worm's reproduction system. After mating, it forms cocoons with fertilized eggs that the worm deposits in the surrounding bedding.

Cocoon /egg
These are small elliptical or egg shaped containers formed by the Clitellum of fertilized worms after they have mated with another worm. One cocoon can contain up to 20 infant worms/hatchlings.

Cutting a worm in half
It is a myth that worms which have been cut in half will survive as two new worms. All the vital organs are in the upper half of the worm's body, which may slightly improve its chance of survival if

the worm gets split into two parts. The lower half of the worm will definitely die. *Never cut a worm in half!*

Dry bedding
If the conditions in the worm bin become too dry, particles of bedding will stick to the skin of the worms and suffocate them.

Feeding rule #1
Never cover the *whole* surface of any worm bin, regardless of its size, with feed. Should there be anything harmful in the materials and it happens to filter down into the bedding you might lose your entire worm-herd.

Feeding rule #2
Grass clippings or plant wastes that have been treated with pesticides can be lethal to your worms and should never be fed to them.

Gloves
Do not work without gloves
Ideally, strong rubber gloves (typically used for dishwashing or gardening), should be used at all times when working with worms as worm eggs/ capsules can become infertile when they come into contact with human skin.

Harvesting worms
Always use a manure fork when you are harvesting or moving worms in bulk beds. You are less likely to injure or kill worms with the manure fork than a spade or shovel.

Hosepipe
It's used to add water to bulk beds, breeder bins, compostable material and worm feed. Keep to a minimum if your tap water contains chlorine.

Lighting
Lights can be hung above breeder boxes to prevent worms from escaping. Mature worms have the habit of migrating out of confined spaces if they feel too crowded. This may typically occur during or after a rainstorm. Worms, although blind, can feel light on their skin and will always try to hide from it.

Manure fork
Manure forks are used to turn compost, harvest worms from bulk beds and feed bulk beds. Ideally, you should use a fork with round prongs.

Moisture level
The ideal moisture level inside a worm bin compares to that of a squeezed out sponge. Take a handful of bedding and squeeze it in your fist. If a few drops of moisture drop down this indicates that the water saturation in the bedding is perfect. A few drops more will still be fine.

Nesting versus stacking bins
Nested bins have slightly sloping sides so that they drop down into the bin beneath to rest on whatever material is in the lower bin. Stacking bins do not sink into the bin beneath, and the walls of the bins are able to rest securely on each other so that they can be stacked one on top of the other.

PH level
Worms can tolerate pH levels from 6 - 8.5 but thrive in a pH neutral environment of about 7.0. Highly acidic bedding can be deadly if worms cannot find a way to escape from it.

PH meter
 This is used to monitor the pH level in worm bins.

Pit run worms
This is another name for worms that live in a bulk bed.

Plastic bag sealer (optional)
These are great for neatly sealing attractive bags of worm castings and other fertilizing mixes. You can also use the much cheaper option of a staple gun and upgrade to a plastic bag sealer later.

Plastic sheeting
Sheeting is essential for low cost bulk beds, setting up certain types of breeder boxes, and covering the surface of breeder boxes and some types of bulk beds. It is also used as a cover for the compost heap during the aerobic composting process.

Power tools
Necessary tools such as a drill and jigsaw are needed to prepare worm bins and buckets for worms.

Scale (optional)
If you prefer to weigh the worms instead of counting them, you can make use of an accurate kitchen or commercial scale.

Scissors
They are used to cut packaging paper, Velcro strips, pallet wrapping and soft plastic sheets, if needed.

Shelving
Shelving or storage space will be required for your bins, buckets, plastic sheets and accessories as well as for worm farms and other products. It does not have to be a massive space. An area of 3 - 5 m² should be sufficient to begin with.

Spade
Used to turn compost and harvest worm castings from bulk beds.

Splitting - or separating worms
This refers to the separation of mature worms from infant worms and cocoons/ eggs in your breeder bins. The mature worms will be replaced in the breeder bin while the infant worms and cocoons will be added to a bulk bed.

Squeeze test
The Squeeze test is an easy way to determine the moisture level of the bedding in a worm farm. Take a handful of bedding and squeeze it in your fist. If a few drops of moisture fall down, it indicates that the water saturation in the bedding is perfect. A few additional drops will still be fine.

Note: Make sure there are no worms in the bedding that you are testing.

Suitable conditions in the bin
Worms are pretty hardy creatures but they need certain environmental conditions to be met in order to live and reproduce inside their worm bin, namely: moderate temperatures (5-28 degrees centigrade), adequate moisture (see squeeze test), oxygen supply (see aeration) and a neutral pH level in the bedding.

Tables
Tables are ideal work surfaces for separating adult worms taken from the breeder boxes from the cocoons and infant worms, for counting worms for sale and for packaging products.

Temperatures
Worms can survive conditions as cold as 5 °C and as hot as 30 °C.
Ideal temperatures are between 15 - 20 °C.
Note: The temperature inside the worm bedding will normally be lower than the surrounding air temperature.

Vermiculture/worm farming
This is a simple way of converting organic materials into nutrient rich soil conditioners with the help of earthworms/composting worms.

Water
Whenever possible avoid using chlorinated water (tap water). Pond or rain water (check the pH levels) is usually better for your worms. If you have to use tap water you can reduce the chlorine content by pouring it into large buckets, open containers or basins at least 24 hours before you use it. This will allow much of the chlorine to evaporate. If you have to add water to your worm bins directly from the tap, try to keep it to a minimum.

Watering can
It is used to add water to breeder boxes and bulk beds.

Wheelbarrow (optional)
This is useful for moving large amounts of harvested worm rich bedding from bulk beds, or to move compost, worm castings and worm food.

Winter bed
This refers to a worm bed that is specially prepared to help worms survive the freezing temperatures of cold winters.

Worm bin, worm box, worm farm
These are several different names for the same thing: A safe place for your worms to stay.

Worm breathing
Worms have no lungs and breathe through their skin. That is why they need a moist environment to live in. They need to be able to slide through it without parts of the bedding sticking to their skin.

Worm bristles
Never try to pull a worm out of hole, a piece of cloth or soil. They have bristles on their upper body which act like barbs on a fish hook and the worm uses them to avoid being pulled out of its hiding place. This process is so effective that many worms will snap in two if you pull too hard.

Worm castings
Worm castings are worm poop, which is probably one of the best soil conditioners and natural plant foods known to man.

Worm food
This can be one or a mix of several organic (waste) materials that can be used to feed worms.

Worm leachate
This is excess liquid that has run through the contents of a worm bin. It is often mistakenly called worm tea.

Worm picker
It's a person that counts worms for packaging or sale.

Worm tea
A highly beneficial brew of chlorine free water, worm castings and molasses that can be used as a foliar spray or a liquid plant food.

Worm weight
It is estimated that 4000 pit run worms (*Eisenia fetida*) weigh about 1kg.

Worms
Eisenia fetida is the species of composting worms referred to in this book.

Worms and the sun
Worms will always flee from any kind of light and will die within a few minutes if exposed to sunlight unless they find a way to hide.

Worms can drown
Although worms can live for extended periods in water they will drown if the water does not contain a lot of oxygen.

CONVERSION TABLES

TEMPERATURE			
Celsius	Fahrenheit	Celsius	Fahrenheit
0	32.00		
1	33.80	21	69.80
2	35.60	22	71.60
3	37.40	23	73.40
4	39.20	24	75.20
5	41.00	25	77.00
6	42.80	26	78.80
7	44.60	27	80.60
8	46.40	28	82.40
9	48.20	29	84.20
10	50.00	30	86.00
11	51.80	31	87.80
12	53.60	32	89.60
13	55.40	33	91.40
14	57.20	34	93.20
15	59.00	35	95.00
16	60.80	36	96.80
17	62.60	37	98.60
18	64.40	38	100.40
19	66.20	39	102.20
20	68.00	40	104.00

LENGTH			
Centimeters	**Inches**	**Centimeters**	**Inches**
1	0.39	21	8.27
2	0.78	22	8.66
3	1.18	23	9.06
4	1.57	24	9.45
5	1.97	25	9.85
6	2.36	26	10.24
7	2.75	27	10.63
8	3.15	28	11.03
9	3.54	29	11.42
10	3.94	30	11.82
11	4.33	31	12.21
12	4.72	32	12.60
13	5.12	33	13.00
14	5.51	34	13.39
15	5.91	35	13.79
16	6.30	36	14.18
17	6.69	37	14.57
18	7.09	38	14.97
19	7.48	39	15.36
20	7.88	40	15.76

LENGTH			
Meters	**Feet**	**Meters**	**Feet**
1	3.28	21	68.88
2	6.56	22	72.16
3	9.84	23	75.44
4	13.12	24	78.72
5	16.40	25	82.00
6	19.68	26	85.28
7	22.96	27	88.56
8	26.24	28	91.84
9	29.52	29	95.12
10	32.80	30	98.40
11	36.08	31	101.68
12	39.36	32	104.96
13	42.64	33	108.24
14	45.92	34	111.52
15	49.20	35	114.80
16	52.48	36	118.08
17	55.76	37	121.36
18	59.04	38	124.64
19	62.32	39	127.92
20	65.60	40	131.20

AREA			
Sq. meters	Sq. feet	Sq. meters	Sq. feet
1	10.76	21	226.06
2	21.52	22	236.82
3	32.29	23	247.59
4	43.05	24	258.35
5	53.82	25	269.12
6	64.58	26	279.88
7	75.35	27	290.65
8	86.11	28	301.41
9	96.88	29	312.18
10	107.64	30	322.94
11	118.41	31	333.71
12	129.17	32	344.47
13	139.94	33	355.24
14	150.70	34	366.00
15	161.47	35	376.77
16	172.23	36	387.53
17	183.00	37	398.30
18	193.76	38	409.06
19	204.53	39	419.83
20	215.29	40	430.59

VOLUME (LIQUID)

Liters	US Gallons	Liters	US Gallons
1	0.26	21	5.56
2	0.52	22	5.82
3	0.79	23	6.09
4	1.05	24	6.35
5	1.32	25	6.62
6	1.58	26	6.88
7	1.85	27	7.15
8	2.11	28	7.41
9	2.38	29	7.68
10	2.64	30	7.94
11	2.91	31	8.21
12	3.17	32	8.47
13	3.44	33	8.74
14	3.70	34	9.00
15	3.97	35	9.27
16	4.23	36	9.53
17	4.50	37	9.80
18	4.76	38	10.06
19	5.03	39	10.33
20	5.29	40	10.59

21431713R00083

Printed in Great Britain
by Amazon